66 Days to Change Your Life: 12 Steps to Effortlessly Remove Mental Blocks, Reprogram Your Brain and Become a Money Magnet

Dan Desmarques

Published by 22 Lions Bookstore, 2019.

Table of Contents

Copyright Page 1

About the Publisher 3

Introduction 5

Why is this Knowledge Important? 7

Why this System Works? 9

Why 66 Days? 11

Why are Habits Difficult to Form? 13

Why Do We Need to Make Sacrifices? 15

Why Rich People Think Differently? 17

Why Do You Need to Change Alone? 19

Why the Facts Don't Matter? 21

Why Nothing is Impossible? 23

Why is Time Relative? 25

Why 21 Days is Not Enough? 27

Why Will Your Social Life Be Affected? 29

Why is Religion Misleading? 31

Why God Punishes the Stupid? 35

What Can You Do about Mass Ignorance? 37

Why is Ignorance the Main Enemy? 39

Why Love is Not the Answer? 41

Why You Don't Need to Predict the Future? 43

Why Losing Relationships is a Good Thing? 45

What is the Real Source of Any Disagreement? 47

The Law of Attraction in a Nutshell 49

Why Affirmations aren't Enough to Create Changes? 51

Your Emotional Relationship With Money 53

Why are Money and Social Status Interrelated? 55

Why Certain Cultural Values Can Keep You Poor? 59

Why Your Friends Can Keep You Poor? 61

The Big Lie in Equalitarianism 63

Step 1: Deprogramming Your Mind 65

Step 2: Removing Money Blocks 67

Step 3: Increasing Your Magnetic Power 81

Step 4: Rehabilitating Your Imagination 85

Step 5: Realigning Your Spirit 87

Step 6: Rewriting Your Karma 89

Step 7: Opening Quantum Gates 95

Step 8: Singing Mantras for Abundance 97

Step 9: Eliminating Negative Beliefs 99

Step 10: Cleaning Your Sexual Energy 103

Step 11: Increasing Your Wealth by Using Karma 107

Step 12: Attracting More Wealth with Love 111

Copyright Page

66 Days to Change Your Life: 12 Steps to Effortlessly Remove Mental Blocks, Reprogram Your Brain and Become a Money Magnet

By Dan Desmarques

Copyright © Dan Desmarques, 2019 (1st Ed.). All Rights Reserved.

Copyright © Dan Desmarques, 2019 (2nd Ed.). All Rights Reserved.

Published by 22 Lions Bookstore and Publishing House

About the Publisher

About the 22 Lions Bookstore:

www.22Lions.com

Facebook.com/22Lions

Twitter.com/22lionsbookshop

Instagram.com/22lionsbookshop

Pinterest.com/22lionsbookshop

Introduction

The main idea for the production of this book appeared after realizing how the beliefs of others were constantly making me lose money and delaying my life in what regards reaching my goals, even leading me to fail in businesses I had just started.

The awareness to this fact was extremely frustrating but also difficult to control for a multitude of reasons, namely, because we can't always detect who such people are, and also because, even when doing so, we may not be able to remove them from our life.

The only way to solve this problem effectively consists in the creation of a system that can rearrange the different patterns of our existence at once and through the focus in one area only, preferably of a material nature, as it is the case with money.

The content presented here comes from the premise that, if our thoughts interfere with our fate, the thoughts of others, operating by default, can have a greater influence over such fate.

Have you ever noticed how happy some people are when you fail, as if they were already expecting it? Or how sympathetic some individuals appear to be when you are poor? They are the same ones resenting your happiness and abundance when you later in life become successful, and then claiming the most absurd things to prove that you are unworthy of what you get, and this, while finding excuses to remove themselves from your reality.

This social paradigm is so obvious, that another, contradicting this common behavior, had to be present too. I found it and later decided to create a system to help me apply it. After seeing immediate results manifesting in my own life, even as I was creating this book — due to the fact that I was reading the exercises in my mind while preparing the content — I concluded that the application of this system would be very useful for the many readers that I have spread all over the globe.

Why is this Knowledge Important?

There are millions of books out there, even courses and videos, on the topic of attracting abundance and wealth, namely, on the law of attraction, vibration and manifestation. There are even groups on this planet with specific therapies to help people overcome their subconscious mind and attract wealth. However, as I came to realize, after studying with many of such groups, the large majority doesn't understand the full spectrum of how the human mind operates, and that's why they usually fail in helping most people, or can only help them obtain what their mind already allowed within its limitations. As a matter of fact, most of what you learn from them, is simply a lie, outdated, common sense or misleading. As useful as such knowledge might be, it will never lead to outstanding results.

Personally, I've always disliked wasting my own time, and even ended friendships and relationships that were stopping me from reaching my life goals, usually facing months of loneliness in the process because of the values that I was certainly not giving up on. And, naturally, it is hard to follow an extreme lifestyle. But you only have one chance at proving your real value in this world. This is why I did my own research based on the most advanced and effective techniques available to reprogram and heal the mind, and then redesigned the strategy presented here for specific purposes, first and foremost, with the intention of using it to achieve my own financial dreams and eliminate any limiting beliefs.

The more I focused on the application of this system, the faster I noticed that the naysayers, the negative personalities and everyone else that opposed my success, kept disappearing from my reality, while those who wanted to be part of it, started to change, becoming more supportive and even, in some cases, helping me achieve the results I wanted.

Only two months had passed, when I noticed that nearly all of my friends were either entrepreneurs or successful artists, just like me.

This is when I realized how deeply wealth is correlated with anything else, even the people we surround ourselves with and how they feel about us.

Finally, as I kept attracting wealthy people into my life, and seeing the ones who hold a poverty mindset, or that don't believe in my success, moving apart, I also saw my path towards my dreams getting clearer, allowing me to become more skillful in obtaining the results I sought, which, on the other hand, attracted even more money in my direction.

This said, I have no doubt that this system is of a tremendous help to me, solving problems that I have tried to clear out of my way throughout my entire existence. And this is why I keep applying it on a daily basis. For this reason, it is my pleasure, as an author and researcher, to now share this system with you.

Why this System Works?

All you need to do to be successful in applying this book, is to wake up early every morning, and repeat the lists of exercises presented here. If you are honest with your work, if you don't suffer from any mental illness, if you're not an alcoholic or have a history of drug abuse, you will most likely see results in a relatively short period of time.

Every person that I know of, who has been applying the knowledge outlined here and in other books about wealth that I authored, has doubled, and even tripled in many cases, their previous income, typically obtaining job offers where they got higher salaries, or starting businesses that allowed them to quit their own daily job. And I've consistently seen such results for the past decade, since I started becoming more popular worldwide with books on the law of attraction and wealth. I have actually made up to twenty times more than I was doing before by applying the same techniques to my own life.

Despite these results, this book takes everything to a higher level, because the purpose here is inward and not outward. Your real purpose with this book is to clean your mind from everything and anything that is stopping you from becoming wealthier, in the premise that you were born wealthy, and any path can guide you there, to your desired goal, especially, if you always felt that the work you've put out, and the many hours in studying about money, didn't allow you to reach it.

This book will surely help you in attracting the wealth that is already destined to your life. And it will manifest itself in various ways, as I've seen in the life of others. If you want a higher salary, you may get a better job offer with the amount you wish to receive; if you're a business owner, you may start seeing sales picking up, or getting ideas that lead you there; and much more. I was personally able to increase my income while creating this book, and just while reading the exercises as I was creating them. My income kept increasing every single month.

I wish the same to you by sharing the secrets outlined here. They are based on an extensive research that I have been applying to my own life and the life of others.

Why 66 Days?

Scientists have come to the conclusion that it requires about 66 days for a person to change a habit; and habits condition our thoughts, which are influenced by the truths we convince ourselves with. These truths then make what we consider to be our "comfort zone" — a set of beliefs that may not serve us well or even help in reaching our goals, even though conditioning our decisions on a daily basis.

It is because our reality is so interconnected with our mind, that we can't change it easily and without consistency. For that, you need a system as the one outlined here.

You see, many habits are familiar to us because they relate to behavior patterns in others that match our own — the same people we typically insist in keeping in our life because of their familiarity. Changing our habits then means facing a change in our environment and resistance from the people we know, and that makes the process much harder than a simple shift of focus.

This is why so many techniques, like affirmations, or even self-hypnosis, have a big risk of failure, as it is much more difficult to make someone else become familiar with a new presence in you, a new attitude, than to create it within yourself; not only do we create the habits that entrap us in a repetitive loop, but also reward ourselves for it; we reward ourselves for those bad habits when we do something pleasant like having a nice dinner in the weekend to compensate for a horrible week of work, when we drink alcohol on a Friday night to have fun and forget the rest of the week, and when we do anything else that helps in releasing ourselves from stress, namely, when fattening ourselves with sugar.

Every time we reward ourselves for a life we hate, to compensate for the negative emotions within us, we reinforce our habits and suppress our awareness, and this while maintaining the same beliefs. That's why thinking positive to compensate for a life you hate is actually a bad thing to do. It means suppressing reality under a layer of delusion, from which all the justifications for not changing emerge.

Despite these facts, studies show that it is possible to break from even the most well built habits, if we maintain a behavior consistency for an average of 66 days.

In a study released by the European Journal of Social Psychology, Phillippa Lally and her team of researchers surveyed 96 people over a 12-week period to find exactly how long it takes to start a new habit. Over the 12 weeks, the participants chose a new habit and reported each day on how automatic the behavior felt. At the end of that period, Lally analyzed the results and found the average time it took for the participants to pick up a new habit was 66 days.

Why are Habits Difficult to Form?

Many experiments show us that habits take time to be accepted by the subconscious mind in order to then to be operated with by default. Needless to say, we keep the strongest habits copied from our parents, due to the many years of living under their rules and behavior patterns. Many of their repetitive phrases are even immersed in our subconscious mind like mantras, controlling our thoughts and beliefs.

It is actually interesting to see how people sabotage their own life by copying habits that don't match their goals, and this, due to an emotional familiarity. If, for example, your parents were alway dramatizing lack of money, and alcohol abuse, you may find yourself drinking too much on the weekends and avoiding well-paid jobs, in order to replicate the same emotions with your spouse. If your mother was always worried about scarcity, and your father wasted most of his money on futilities, you may find yourself subconsciously attracted to the same behavior patterns on a partner, and wasting your money on things you don't need — like your father did, in order to be as worried at the end of the month as your mothers was.

A large amount of our habits come from emotional patterns and interrelated beliefs, deeply rooted in our subconscious mind. In order to change them, we must rethink our identity — the personality we have been accustomed to feel and represent to others. It would be like doing a plastic surgery and then having to face our relatives, friends and coworkers with a completely new face, that doesn't, in any way, resemble our previous one or their own.

If you want to be more drastic about this impact or any other important change, just consider how mentally affected others would be if you decided to change gender. Because, you see, a change of gender won't affect the people around you as much as becoming much wealthier than they are ever will.

Becoming wealthier is like growing to a point in which others can only see a shadow of your previous self, a shadow that covers their egotistic mindset and makes them look at themselves from a lower perspective by comparison to yours. And jealousy is a very powerful, primitive, but also instinctive, response to social changes. The wider the gap of such changes, the more you will awake hatred, fear and resentment towards you. As a result, you end up attracting animosity and criticism too.

Whenever changing yourself, you need to be prepared for the adjustments in your social interactions, for they will happen, even against your will. These adjustments will force you to question yourself, delay any accomplishment and, if you allow it, sabotage your potential for success.

Why Do We Need to Make Sacrifices?

One of the most interesting things that people do, whenever they perceive that you are changing before their eyes, is to make you doubt your own potential in reaching your dreams, by stressing the importance of your weaknesses and background, as if rooting you back into failure patterns.

Anything goes when someone is trying to break you, especially, when they are afraid to lose you or have something to gain from doing it. One of my former girlfriends, for example, used racism, my nationality, and even the average level of intelligence of my family, to stop me from becoming a successful author. I was forced to end the relationship with her, along with the possibility of any marriage, and change country, because there was no other way I could succeed with such person in my life, singing the same mantras every day. It was like living with a disease.

Many of my friends used materialistic facts, namely, my low income in the beginning, to make me believe that I couldn't transform that into a thousand times more. But if you live in Europe, even the resentful stare of tourists and locals will make you question the legality, normality and validity of what you do. Because, surely, once they notice that you don't have, and don't need, a job, and can sit in front of the beach with a laptop drinking orange juice whenever you want, the sense of unfairness awakens within them. I even remember a North American girl telling me at the gym: "You should never tell anyone that you don't have a job."

She was right, because every time I told any other girl in Spain that I was an author, she would avoid me. Some, in Lithuania, would even tell me: "I wouldn't stop dating you even if you did something illegal, like selling drugs".

One way or another, I was perceived as abnormal. And humans always correlate what is abnormal with illegal or dangerous.

When I finally had a Lithuanian girlfriend, it was her family and friends who started insulting me. The first one to resent my social status, was her pathetic brother, who despite being an IT professional, did not know how to work on his own. "Your boyfriend is an important drug lord in disguise, as nobody can make money from books", He said once at the dinner table.

You will be surprised at how stupid many people, in some cases, who appear to be intelligent, really are, and how insulting they can be, due to the simple fact that they are ignorant about the whole world and its mechanics.

This is one of the many reasons why so many secrets are kept hidden from the masses, most of which in plain sight, through allegories, symbols and metaphysical descriptions that, quite simply, are not accessible to the unprepared minds of the majority. By hiding the truth in lawyers of abstraction and complexity, the masses were kept in the dark for thousand of years. For, otherwise, the self-destructive impact of their actions would be greater than the common insulting of others who know better than them.

It is then when you can't keep or get a new relationship, or even a friendship, when everyone hates you for being better than they are, when even locals stare at you and talk to you as if you were a criminal, an outcast, and you spend a large portion of your time either alone or being invalidated in awkward conversations — that start with random questions and end up with you, basically, trying to prove why you deserve to be alive— that you start seriously questioning the validity of your dreams. And yet, as you keep moving forward, and setting yourself apart from a heard's mentality, you will also naturally attract more situations alike, more people that experience the same as you do, and think like you.

The system presented here is not miraculous, for it intends to simply accelerate this process.

Why Rich People Think Differently?

The only situations where you can be respected for your success, by those who have a sheep mentality and a self-defeating mindset operating by default, is on a stage, on television or when a gun is pointing at their head. That's why respect is either attributed to fear or fame. And that's why I confuse people, as they can't find me either self-promoting myself or being associated with criminal activities. And yet, they always imagine something accordingly, to justify their ignorance and emotional predisposition to the mental states I mentioned.

It doesn't matter how many best selling titles I have, because only when I post a photo of myself talking to a crowd, do I receive appreciation, either from readers or friends. Likewise, it doesn't matter how many awards I have as a musician, because I am only praised and admired whenever posting videos of myself performing in public to a crowd of thousands of people.

The large majority of human beings, no matter which level of education or socioeconomic status they may possess, only respect fear (i.e., threats to their physical survival) and power (i.e., intimidation and social influence). And there is nothing you can do to change that, for they are, in various degrees, wired to be within a "prey or preyer" mentality.

In this sense, you can't be rich if you can't keep a personality to match it; one which, basically, is constantly at war with the outside world. And that is why studies, such as the ones conducted by Professor Peter Belmi, from the University of Virginia have proven that people born into higher social classes are more overconfident and have "an exaggerated belief" that they will perform better than others, as opposed to those in lower classes.

That overconfidence, naturally, demands a certain dose of assertiveness that requires training, because the masses fear overconfidence. That is why I am stopped and carefully checked in every single airport I pass, for no other reason than, according to the security guards themselves, "Appearing suspicious", whatever that means to them.

I was once approached by three security guards in Lithuania, who demanded to see my passport, because, according to them, I was there "reading a book for three hours during a weekday in a public coffee shop, and that is very strange and suspicious".

It is amazing how accurate some movies are about our reality, because indeed, as Morpheus said in the Matrix, "You have to understand, most of these people are not ready to be unplugged. And many of them are so inured, so hopelessly dependent on the system, that they will fight to protect it".

In other words, if you don't like the system and try to escape it, you become a threat to the system itself, and everyone else that needs it to survive. Your changes literally represent a threat to their existence. This is why they act in weird ways and say the most unbelievable things, even when being complete strangers to you. People will literally commit crimes and abuse the legal system to prove you are a criminal.

That is how ignorant of their ignorance the large majority is. They live in a very tiny world of their own. It is not the real world but the one they have chosen to believe in and die for; and they will not respect you for escaping such world.

One of my former girlfriends used to tell me that, if I was famous, I would be much richer, because she actually believed in the correlation between social influence and money, and did not realize how famous I already am with my work. She also doesn't know that social influence isn't related to money, but perceptions.

The truth is that I am extremely famous for many years already, but just not openly exposing myself, as whenever I did that, what I actually got wasn't more profit, but more threats and attempts at removing my books from the market. And this, for the reasons exposed here. For the more impact you have, the scarier people will be.

Why Do You Need to Change Alone?

The phenomenon that a drastic change represents is so interesting that, the first time I created it, was when I was only about 16yo and by accident. I was a bad student up until that point, suffering from what is now considered hyperactivity; plus, I had a horrible memory that wouldn't allow me to remember anything I read or listen. My mother even assumed that I was probably autistic.

I seemed destined to a miserable future, and my parents kept reminding me of such fate by telling me what a loser I was. But somehow, I prayed to God for help and the answers came to me, in the form of intuitive guidance.

I followed that inner voice, and did things I never considered before, for I had never seen anyone doing them anyway. That included searching for different school manuals to compare them, including the ones still owned by my grandfather and that he himself used when he was a student.

I also started reading encyclopedias on psychology at the same time. I would devour anything related to the mind, intelligence, emotions, and learning.

Why I did that, I can't really precise, as I was still a teenager, and simply being guided by that inner spiritual voice. It would tell me first to study in the library instead of bringing the manuals home, and then, as I was reading, it would instruct me, by saying, "Go see if there is a book you would like to read for fun". And, as I was passing through the different bookshelves, that voice would stop me with a "Here". I would then look at the shelf in front of me to know why, and that's when I would see books with the exact answers I needed.

I was so in love with knowledge that I devoured everything I could find from what was being presented to me. And soon after I started applying the techniques learned from those books.

I went from being the worse student in the whole school, often perceived as retarded, even by my own parents, to being the best. In just a few months, I would surpass all the top students. And this experience was so astonishing to my teachers that they refused to believe. Many times they repeated exams because they felt the results weren't "fair". For I was beating all the top students.

Many teachers kept a close attention on me, looking for an extraordinary method of cheating that was impossible to detect. Many of them would literally stand next to me during the exams, ignoring the rest of the class, to observe me for an entire hour without taking their eyes from my hands. They were astonished and refusing to believe what was happening before them.

This situation would repeat later in my life as family members started suspecting I was involved in criminal activities in China, for I was traveling the world without a fixed job, while working for a minimum wage as a teacher once in a while.

After becoming the best student in high school, many of my previous friends resented it and stopped talking to me. I somehow stopped belonging to their "circle of ignorance" and made them feel bad with themselves. The more I tried to explain myself, by actually sharing my techniques, the worse it was. They refused to believe in the hard work I was putting to learn from different books, and the vast amount of hours I was spending to acquire knowledge, by waking up at 4AM, many hours before going to school, to study, or the fact that I was spending entire weekends doing the same.

They refused to believe because, to believe, implied accepting their own responsibility for their own fate, and that's something most people can't accept in any stage of their life. I have even lost many friends in recent years by telling them the answers that their psychologists couldn't or would somehow never give.

Quite simply, people want to be accepted, not changed.

Why the Facts Don't Matter?

The IQ test results, given by the school psychologist, proved that I was stupid, but that didn't stop me and didn't matter to me anymore at that point. And yet, interestingly, stopped those who considered themselves smarter than me from following my teachings and research conclusions. Many kept believing I was either lucky or cheating.

This situation would also repeat itself later in my adult life, for many people don't think they should be learning from me because I don't drive Lamborghinis or own the mansions which they consider to justify listening to anyone.

However, losing friendships wasn't worse than being insulted at home. My parents went from "having a stupid son" to "having a stupid son that was now acting like an autistic teenager, closing himself and reading books alone like some psycho from horror movies."

That was the moment when my mother got so paranoid — especially, when seeing the amount of notes that I was writing, based on observations and personal researches — that she decided to hire a psychiatrist, and later a psychologist, to evaluate me.

As I believe now, this is where a rupture between the past and the future shows itself, because the more my parents tried to stop me from changing, the more their life changed for worse. My mother ended up meeting a childhood friend that was going through a divorce, fell in love with him again and dumped my father, who in his loneliness and despair started dating someone else, and leaving me alone too.

The window of opportunity grew larger, and I never spoke to them again. I did have to go through a hard period of loneliness and even live as a homeless teenager, but I guess I had turned too smart at that point to fail again, as even the psychologists and psychiatrists I encountered supported me and helped me reach my goals, despite what my mother would tell them to make me seem psychopathic.

You can't beat science with arguments, and every single brain scan and personality test I did, proved that I was healthier than most people doing the same tests. No doctor or therapist could deny those facts.

The funny thing is that, if I had done those same tests ten years earlier, they would probably prove my mother right. For I did not just change my level of intelligence, but my whole DNA in the process too, with techniques that I was researching on spirituality.

If I had focused on the facts, I would not have accomplished the impossible.

Why Nothing is Impossible?

The stories of my past would end up repeating themselves later in my life, when any woman who attempted to stop me from writing books and becoming wealthier, would somehow meet a man that fooled her into leaving me. Thanks to that, they were removed from my reality, and I ended up in better situations than what I was considering possible before they left.

Due to my determination, I always became richer, and all barriers, in any shape or form, kept being removed from my path. Whenever I felt stuck, lacking hope or opportunities, I merely increased my focus in God, and the impossible was made possible before anyone who could not believe it.

These changes would never manifest if I had allowed my emotions to control me. But I cannot say that it isn't extremely painful to accept such changes within us. What I am really saying is that, the most important, painful and drastic changes in our life, always occur within us. You have to be willing to love and let go, attach and detach, embrace and quit, learn and unlearn, and even help the ones who may betray you. There is no other way.

You do grow stronger with those experiences. Even the most chaotic experiences and the most evil of humans force you to remove the deepest fears in you. And which ones are those? They are the fear of humiliation, betrayal, poverty, loneliness and abandonment. Once you conquer these, nothing will scare you anymore. But you won't know how strong you are until you face them.

Good people will never put you through such despair. That's why evil is always a necessary evil.

If you look at any evil or barrier as a test to your faith and self-belief, nothing can ever stop you. And this, because anything in this world, including the experiences you encounter, are illusions to test your faith.

Why is Time Relative?

The amount of time necessary, to see opportunities that weren't previously available to you, depends on many factors. And you never change as much as others change towards you. Just consider that it is as easy to move from your current reality to a new one, as it is to fool someone, who doesn't want that to happen, into leaving you alone and allowing you to succeed, and especially when such person thinks that she is doing the opposite.

Surely, a woman who cheats on her partner, who is trying to be rich, by leaving him for a richer man, believes that she is succeeding; but only until that new man abandons her, and she realizes that it is too late to go back to the previous man, who is now much richer than before. And this, thanks to the fact that she left him for long enough for him to accomplish his goals.

We never know how one situation leads to another, until we look back and see all the patterns combining themselves amidst a chaos. Most of our decisions are never truly ours, but within the paradigm described, we do achieve our goals, if we keep ourselves focused on what we really want.

The example previously mentioned came from my own life and occurred twice, reason why I can only be thankful to the two women who cheated when I needed their emotional support the most. By detaching from my life, they forced me to shift from that emotional neediness towards a stronger self-belief and a higher faith in God. If they had not done it, I would probably marry them, and never reach my goals.

As I came to understand, through different struggles and moments of despair, you don't really need time or large amounts of money to make important decisions. What you do need is the exact opportunity, at the right moment, and enough money to take it, which may even come to you in unexpected ways if you don't already have it.

Fear is never an option, for God knows what awaits you, when you're able to cross the wall of insecurities and embrace the opportunities that are given to you to accomplish your best. For this reason, I am not afraid anymore to make difficult decisions. What I do fear is the lack of faith in others. Whenever I associate myself with a person that has no faith, either in business or in a relationship, I am more likely to fail by association.

Most people don't only lack faith but also a basic understanding of themselves and their capacity to change. They tend to overestimate themselves far too much while underestimating others, especially, when feeling entitled to large amounts of money. Quire frankly, most of the people I have encountered during my entire life, don't even deserve the jobs they have, much less their salaries. The fact that they think I am lucky, for not needing a job, proves my point. For luck is created and deserved.

Why 21 Days is Not Enough?

Many experiments led people to believe that 15 to 21 days was the required period for a change of habits. That, however, is only the starting point of any change.

This belief emerged from certain experiments on medicine and plastic surgery. Maxwell Maltz, a plastic surgeon in the 1950s, began noticing a strange pattern among his patients. When he would perform an operation — like a nose job, for example — he found that it would take the patient about 21 days to get used to seeing their new face. Similarly, when a patient had an arm or a leg amputated, he noticed that the patient would sense a phantom limb for about 21 days before adjusting to the new situation. And these experiences prompted Maltz to think about his own adjustment period to changes and new behaviors as he noticed that it also took himself about 21 days to form a new habit.

Maltz then wrote about these experiences and said: "These, and many other commonly observed phenomena tend to show that it requires a minimum of about 21 days for an old mental image to dissolve and a new one to jell."

In the decades that followed, Maltz's results influenced nearly every major "self-help" author and guru, but they forgot that he stated "a minimum of about 21 days" and not that "it takes 21 days to form a new habit"; and that's how the myth of the 21 to 30 days begun.

How long it takes to a new habit to form can vary, depending on the type of change that is required and the circumstances around the person, as mentioned before. That is why many other studies show us that it can take anywhere from 18 to 254 days for people to form a new habit.

To be more realistic, depending on your efforts and the habit you want to change, it may take you anywhere from two to eight months, to build a new behavior pattern, and not simply 15, 21 or even 30 days. Therefore, although 21 days is the minimum, and 66 days is the average, we don't really know, and can't precisely conclude, from all the experiments conducted, how long it takes for a person in particular to change a habit. What we do know is that you need, most likely, 66 days, to change mental patterns, and to adapt to a new version of yourself, one which can guarantee you better results in life.

This said, what this book proposes you is the responsibility in taking care of your mind with a specific path that you must follow for, at least, 66 days minimum, in order to witness changes occurring. But, naturally, the longer you apply it, the better it is for you.

There isn't any counter effect here, and you can never apply these techniques for too long. There are only positive outcomes to extract from this process.

As money is related to your success and life goals, your personality, your health, your social life, and everything else that can be related to it will change in the process. Your life, generally speaking, will become better.

Why Will Your Social Life Be Affected?

Since I started applying the system outlined here, plenty of people whom I considered to be good friends, started insulting me for no apparent reason. It is actually very intriguing to witness it, as the ones who have a poor mindset, or want to see you poor —sometimes, just because they think rich people are evil (and many people I met do think I'm evil for no other reason than attracting money easily) — when you work on yourself, start insulting you and basically "blowing up emotional grenades", making it easier for you to detach from them, as they themselves do all the work of cutting themselves off from your reality.

You then notice other people appearing in your life. For example, a girl I met three years ago, started sending me huge texts and talking to me about several topics when I started applying this system, and out of nowhere. She is from a very wealthy family. But more interesting than that, is that one of her friends, who is also from a wealthy family herself, was the only one showing interest in me among all the women I encountered in the past months, and after my former girlfriend decided to remove herself from my life, by associating herself with friends who are poor and were destroying the relationship. She chose to end the relationship instead of those friendships, and in doing so redesigned her fate, while opening space in my life for someone better to come along. She moved to a tiny room, sharing the house with other three people, and I decided to travel the world on my own, and enjoy life by myself. I could have been enjoying it with her by my side, but she made her choice very clearly, when soon after she moved to a new relationship, even if it did not last too long. But poor people always make poor decisions.

These type of coincidences show us how the law of attraction is always operating in front os us and through us. It is with such events, for better or for worse, that you will see which theories are based on facts and, therefore, applicable.

This is why, for me, life itself is my laboratory. I know that my knowledge is real because I live it. And it wouldn't make sense for me if it wasn't so, or if my readers did not prove me right, with their own life experience as well.

Most people I encounter seriously underestimate the power of my knowledge, and that's why I must tell you that, a big portion of my readers, are either doctors, members of secret societies, or both. This pattern was a surprise to me as much as for anyone else, but it is indeed a constant, even though I thought I was writing for common people. The truth is that common people will never see or understand this information. It is too complex and far from their limited mind.

You see, even if the level of my work is kept simple and straightforward, the masses don't really understand the complexity of the explanations, and don't even possess the willingness to go as far as to transform their fate in the way proposed here. You need to be different, in a very special way, to be willing to go that far.

Changes are possible, but taking into consideration that the woman in my example lived with me for three years, I must tell you that stupidity is a trait that can last forever, no matter the circumstances or opportunities presented. If she was living next to God, she would still be wasting her time.

Many people are alive, but very few know the meaning of life.

Why is Religion Misleading?

I have friends in many religious groups, and always had, but the Jehovah Witnesses are truly the most damaging ones, among those I have encountered. They seem very friendly, until the opportunity arises to unleash a bunch of imbecility, and out of nowhere, as if they were feeding on the beliefs expressed before that happens.

The last one I met, for example, first asked me for my latest book, and then said he wanted to talk to me. He did, as many others, a kind of "ambush on my brain". He started first by insulting me on the book, saying that I combine too many topics — which is another way of saying that he is too stupid to understand the relation of all things mentioned — as if saying that I don't know what I'm talking about. He then proceeded to ask me if I have rich friends, once again, trying to prove me that I'm too stupid and invent things, and to which I replied, "I don't, not right now, at least."

He laughed at that answer. And well, yes, I don't know any rich friend right now, because I am always working and I'm not investigating how much money my friends really have. I have many friends who are successful business owners, doctors and engineers, or simply born in wealthy families, but if they themselves are rich or poor, I don't truly know, I don't have access to their bank account, and I'm not trying to know either.

Wealth is not measured like that, and there isn't such a thing as a concrete number to wealth. Besides, it's also not something that changes my perspective of others in any way. I do tend to attract the wealthiest people to my life, because the poorest don't identify with what I say, and often insult my words. That is why the majority of my friends, wherever I go in the world, from the United States, to India, China and the European Union, are business owners. They feel attracted to talking to me and spending time with me, and they admire me and respect me, and want to learn from me. They commonly listen to my recommendations on how to improve their business, and also specifically ask for that.

Why they do that? Because they see something in me that, clearly, the idiots and the poor, and those who are destined to fail, cannot see. But that is a coincidence created by my own mindset. And so, it is not as important to say that I have rich friends, as it is to say that I have a rich mindset, which only vibrates on the same frequency of people with a similar mindset.

Now, whatsoever was his intention, due to my respect for him, I wasn't seeing where he was going with this, despite the fact that he was being disrespectful towards my work. But he then continued, using the bible to prove me that God doesn't like the wealthy. And that is a common misunderstanding, proven wrong by several famous scholars.

This said, at that point, I confronted him with his ignorance, by asking, "What are you really trying to say?"

That is when he said that I work too much and money is not as important as I believe. And, I don't like to insult people, but their stupidity is often too insulting to me, because — and here comes the paradox — he was calling me online from a room in Ukraine that he was sharing with six other men.

Taking into account that he is a business owner, and told me many times that his partners cheated on him and even robbed him, and that he is also over 40yo and single, it was a very strong belief for someone that, quite simply, is a complete loser in life.

Here we have a poor, overweight and single, business owner from Mexico, telling me that money is not important, from a room shared with six other men, and surprised with the fact that no woman from his own religion wants to be with him, no matter how many times a day he prays for it, or how many countries he visits every year to find one.

This man has been living in shared rooms all over Europe, Russia, the Middle-East and North Africa, for the past years, and doesn't seem to either be capable of improving his finances or find a woman, but insists in his own beliefs. And worse than that, wants me to believe too, so that maybe he can have more people sharing his misery.

66 DAYS TO CHANGE YOUR LIFE

Last time I visited Ukraine, I rented a whole apartment for myself, and was paying for two during nearly two months, considering the one I left empty behind me in another country. I also met several attractive and intelligent women who were interested in being with me, for either just sex or marriage, while having others interested in the same in other countries, many of whom were contacting me from as far as Asia and North America. That's how powerful my magnetism is. But he dares telling me that I am wrong, and that my books have no particular meaning or purpose.

There is a biblical quote addressing people like him, that says the following: "Give not that which is holy unto the dogs, neither cast ye your pearls before swine, lest they trample them under their feet, and turn again and rend you" (Matthew 7:6).

I do understand that people want to save money. And they should do that as much as possible. But living in a room shared with six other men for nearly a year, and telling someone else that money is not important, is not an honest behavior, much less moral or spiritual. And so, instead of insulting him, I ended the conversation by asking back: "Can you teach me how to ask your God to pay my rent?"

That was enough for him to quit, like the weak, ignorant and pathetic loser he is, and never contact me again. But, nevertheless, he did continue on believing that he was right, despite all evidence in his own life that he was not.

You see, most people fail to understand that religion is created to understand God, and not for God to fit in among them. The Universal Truth does not depend on faith to exist, and is not bound to one religion in particular. And, if God sends someone like me to Earth, and I am ignored, either because I don't lead a religion or accept the religion of others, then that is an insult to God Himself, and no religion can protect the ignorant from the consequences of his lack of humility.

This man continued on believing that he was right, and never recognized that he wasn't, neither did he apologize for his stupidity, but kept sending me messages that I stopped replying.

Personally, I could only feel amazed at how fast my techniques to remove money blocks were working, for I had just made someone — whom I believed was an honest friend — remove himself and his poverty mindset from my life without much effort.

Why God Punishes the Stupid?

Not long ago, I had another disagreement with that same Christian, because he said that God doesn't punish people. I wanted to tell him that God is punishing him for being stupid. But, so many times, by not insulting, I ended up witnessing people doing worse shows of arrogance than I would expect. And well, not surprisingly, he called me arrogant too, which I find interesting, as people do tend to reflect what they see in others. And yet, he did it indirectly, by asking: "What would you feel if I said that you are arrogant?"

I answered him: "I would feel that you don't know me well enough".

He laughed.

Here we have a South American business owner, trying to save money, living in Ukraine and traveling throughout the world, from Europe to Russia, including North Africa, to find a wife, and even the women from his congregation don't want him, because, in general, women don't like men without money. And yet, he is telling me, from his tiny room, shared with six other men, that money is not important and I'm the one who is arrogant and deluded.

This example proves many more things as well, namely, that the law of attraction works without much efforts. Because, you see, I have been insulted so many times already, despite the ones insulting me knowing about the amount of books I wrote, that I don't even care anymore.

As I came to realize, such people are in a kind of trance, and when confronted, always runaway like little scared children. But, it's really interesting to watch how religion manifests in their life. For here we have a man being punished for being stupid, and not understanding why his prayers don't work. They do work, but God won't show Himself amidst ignorance camouflaged by arrogance. He is the one who is arrogant.

I could draw a parallel to this story with the many people who want me to deny what I write, in order to agree with them, as if what I write was invented. I actually wish I had more time to read, but as I said to a friend, I don't really have much more to learn or write; not due to arrogance, but simply because I'm not surprised anymore by what I learn. This is why I tend to move towards topics of higher complexity.

Nonetheless, my latest books are getting much more pages than the previous, because of all these stories. Every time someone insults me, I basically take the experience into a book, to explain my perspective in a more realistic way.

The saddest part for me, personally, is that even though I can understand insults from someone I just met, it's very disappointing to be insulted by someone I know for years already, or that at least talked to me many times about many topics, enough to justify some respect. They make me feel as if they were not really talking to me, but their imaginary version of me inside their own head.

It is because of them that I realized the need to remove money blocks from my own mind, as surely, such blocks attract them to me. They are the living proof that I have money blocks, otherwise I would not even meet them.

People are only attracted to us through the familiarity of patterns inside our mind, which then reflect in our energy field. And, what other people think of us, do affect our results. Firstly, because they usually don't show us what they think, and secondly, because they insist on changing us with vicious tactics like the ones mentioned, just to prove themselves right and us wrong.

Despite these facts, religious members tend to forget that the purpose of religion it to seek God and not to force God to seek them and approve them. Whenever Divine Law is violated, God abandons whoever proceeds with such violation.

What Can You Do about Mass Ignorance?

It is really unbelievable when nothing grants us respect. I mean, it doesn't matter how many people read my books, it doesn't matter if they are mostly doctors or followers of different but important religions, it doesn't matter if I was a college lecturer in the past and for many years, or even if I write books based on my own research and the researches of others; nothing truly matters to someone who has created a prefixed mental image in his head and acts accordingly; an image of what I represent to him; and then refuses to change it, but wants to force me to match it.

There is nothing more arrogant, infantile and psychopathic than this — to force others into matching our version of reality and themselves. That's exactly what separates a religion from a dangerous cult ruled with narcissistic abuses.

The reason why these groups of mass madness attract so many followers — eight million at the present moment — is because, generally speaking, people truly believe, that what is in their mind, about others or reality itself, is the truth, and in doing so, they completely disregard facts and observations. It is a form of mental retardation, even though we often attribute to it more friendly terms, such as lack of consciousness.

I don't consider myself a rude person, or even evil, and much less arrogant, since I share everything I know with the rest of humanity, and do my best to be in good terms with everyone I meet, but it is really hard to handle so much stupidity. It is even harder, when you encounter imbecility in a large group. You can't possibly fight and win against imbecility manifested in such a large scale.

The group mindset convinces everyone that they are right, and that disagreeing means being wrong. That's when their "version of God" or "reality" ends up being more real to them than "reality itself" or the truth. Truth is often denied to match the group's mindset.

Most people are in such a state of trance, that they are like living dead; they are not truly alive. They don't see what they are doing. They are blind to the world in which they live, which ends up becoming nothing more than shadows projected from within their mind. And they then erase any sense of responsibility from within themselves too, to compensate for all that.

These individuals believe they know reality, but their reality is actually a mass schizophrenic manifestation supported by shadowing reflections of their own thoughts.

Why is Ignorance the Main Enemy?

I am very careful about what I write, as I don't lie in my books, and I would be ashamed to tell a person that money is not important while living in a shared room in Kiev. I can teach how to attract money and miracles because I have done it times enough to control the mechanism. But to say that money is not important, is to insult the intelligence of my readers and friends; and I also believe, it is an insult to God Himself.

Imagine that a person tells you: "What you tell me is not important". What would you do? You stop talking to that person. But now you want to offer a thousand euros to that same person, and he says: "Money is not important". What is your reaction to this attitude? You answer him: "Well then, as I don't like to waste my money, I will just give it to someone else."

As you see, it's not hard to understand how God operates and how people misinterpret religion, because these same people talk to God as if saying: "Money is not important but can you please borrow me some?"

What would you think of a person that talks like this to you? You would say: "You are insane; why should I give you money, if you just said you don't need it?"

My point is, anyone with a healthy mindset can easily comprehend how God operates, and how life works, simply by following logic. But when you allow your ability to think to be hijacked by a whole group of debilitated minds, you easily fall into a mass schizophrenia by default. That's why I wrote in some of my books that maybe I should create my own religion, as it seems that this world is completely lost.

People today are in such a state of insanity, that their spiritual beliefs don't really matter anymore. They don't, and can't, understand anymore their own books, much less have a normal conversation with other human beings without the need to prey on their brain like a mad zombie from an apocalyptic movie.

Isn't it paradoxically intriguing when a religion talks about the enemy while not knowing that they themselves are the enemy? It reminds me of those who are possessed by demons and put huge efforts to prove to anyone else that I am evil. It's a waste of time to talk to someone who is not good in the head. "To argue with a person who has renounced the use of reason is like administering medicine to the dead" (Thomas Paine).

Why Love is Not the Answer?

What I mentioned previously about friendships and religion, applies to love as well. You can't possibly win in an argument with a spouse who insists on pulling the "rope of the relationship" on the opposite direction. It breaks apart. And you can't agree unless you are willing to see your dreams shattered to pieces.

The story of my latest relationship forced me to rethink my values and my fears. Because, you see, I don't like to spend so much time alone, as I often do, because of my work and lifestyle. Being an author of extremely complex topics, forces me to spend a huge amount of hours doing research and writing nonstop, which is extremely mentally exhausting and leaves me without much energy for anything else. And I also don't have patience to seek for a new girlfriend and go out all the time. On the other hand, I don't want to be poor or live with someone who is clearly competing against me, and trying to ruin my results. I have seen this too many times. And if a woman is hypergamous, then what this woman is really doing is sabotaging the relationship by bringing me down while I uplift her life, up to a point in which her nagging and frustration expands, and she sees moving on to another relationship as the only solution naturally possible. That's exactly what she did, even if her new adventure lasted less than a month.

You can't beat human nature with logic. Whoever does that is seriously deceiving himself. But you also can't expect the future to be any different from what someone's behavior patterns already shows you. You don't even need a fortuneteller to help you see the obvious. Whoever is driving you down, is already betraying you. The lack of respect for your values is a clear indicator that this person has no empathy for your suffering and won't even blink upon the opportunity to make a selfish decision that will damage you.

In a way, I should feel proud of myself for the fact that a woman who is nearly twenty years younger than me can't find a better man, but I also can't wait around for that to happen. You can actually predict any possible future by looking, not just at words, but the whole spectrum of sentences someone uses, and especially, if many have been identified by experts and famous authors as common to certain personality traits and mental illnesses.

You can't try to control someone's life and your own at the same time either. But it would be foolish to leave a relationship to chance when you already know how it is going to end. It would be like taking your hands from the wheel when driving a car and expect that vehicle to miraculously keep itself on the road.

Why You Don't Need to Predict the Future?

It is strange, when someone you meet in one country ten years before and another person you meet in a new country years later, repeat the exact same sentence, word by word, as if reading a movie script; and it is even more strange, when you learn from experience— and by studying and reading books about certain personalties — that you can then predict the future of such people before they themselves can do that; In fact, this phenomenon is so weird, that I often find myself predicting future events in many people's life just by looking at their behavior patterns. Because, you see, the vast majority is not aware of these things and I don't think they want to be either.

Life becomes very boring and frustrating when you already know the next episode and even the whole season of series of someone in your life; and yet, no matter how much you try to change it, you can't. You can only play inside that movie or refuse to participate.

Most people are so unaware of themselves, that they will never change their course of actions, not even when they see you being right about everyone else around them.

In a recent case that I experienced, I actually read the thoughts and predicted the future of every single friend a girl had, but, because she knew many of them since early childhood, and I had just seen them for a coupe of seconds, she assumed I was crazy. Three years later, however, everything I said was proven true.

This same girl also ended up in a hospital because of a cyst, after I told her that this would occur if she kept smoking marijuana. Instead of stopping, she fought back my arguments with all the nonsense she could find to ridicule me. And once that occurred, she did stop smoking marijuana, but decided to then smoke cigars.

Should I then continue, by telling her that she is now attracting cancer? How could I even do that, when she argues that smoking cigars helps her in losing weight?

It doesn't matter how much you know, or even if you have telepathic and fortunetelling abilities, for a stupid person will always waste your time.

When this girl later shown interest in being in a relationship with me, I told her that I wasn't interested in being with someone who will very likely die within ten years. She felt offended and said she didn't want to be with a man that wishes her death. But on the contrary, my words had the exact opposite intention.

Helping a very stupid human being, is like being a fly inside a spiderweb trying to convince the spider that the web is not well-built. For the spider, all flies are the same, and a web that doesn't catch one may still catch another.

It is very ironic that the more you know, the more everyone will appear to be stupid, and the more they will doubt whatsoever you say, because you will seem crazy to them. That's why the most famous publics speakers are actually not the best, but the ones who most resemble the mental patterns of the majority. And that's why I don't have much consideration or sympathy for any of them.

I know that the truly best won't easily become accepted and assimilated by the masses. In fact, the better my books become, the more any popular self-help book out there looks to me like the work of a storytelling author for kindergarten children.

Why Losing Relationships is a Good Thing?

The majority is not aware of why they do what they do, and is constantly creating their own movies, and forcing others to play specific roles in them, while disrespecting those who refuse to follow the script, as if creating a future by reinforcing specific behavior patterns in the present.

This Earthly trait can be compared to a situation in which you are explaining to an actor that he has free will in the movie he has chosen to participate in, but the actor denies it, and insists on playing the script. Moreover, he doesn't even know he is an actor of the movie anymore. Not only the actor has amnesia in what regards his purpose, but is also unaware of the differences between a movie and reality, i.e., imagination and truth. Moreover, the actor resents you for showing him that fact.

This explains why, when famous actors play psychopathic roles in movies, many of them go insane or fall into a depression.

It is very difficult for a human being to have a detached awareness, because everything else is connected to it. If you lose the movie, you lose your coworkers in that movie too, i.e., your friends' and relatives' respect.

In my relationships, often comes a point in which my only choice is to give ultimatums, such as, "You either stop talking to A and B, or I'll be gone from your life". And, obviously, I make myself look even crazier by saying that. Because the more detached you are from the imaginary world of the majority, the more you will be perceived as being insane by them. It's a natural response of human beings to anything that doesn't fit their preconceived sense of reality.

One could then assume that psychology would solve this problem, but such isn't the case with the large majority, for many psychologists are they themselves insane too. When I told my former girlfriend to see one, that psychologist she found told her the following: "Your boyfriend is trying to control you because you have the right to party alone and get drunk, or talk to former boyfriends and make your own decisions, even if it includes ending his trust on you, and it's his problem if he doesn't agree with you and acts as if he is insecure."

It is really difficult to beat such argument, but who is controlling who here? I'm not even getting paid fifty dollars an hour for my opinion, but instead insulted for showing theories with thousands of years of evidence and logic.

For such people, the fact that I authored over three hundred books, amounts to nothing more than peanuts in comparison to the opinion of a psychologist, who, basically, gets paid to say whatever she wants, without the need to prove it, or obtain results that match the initial intention of the one in therapy.

It is like going to a physician to cure diarrhea and get your head chopped off with your consent. And yet, this is exactly what is occurring in the world right now; people are being mentally raped and spiritually butchered by those they trust the most. Love can't save them from such fate.

It comes a point where I need to make drastic decisions to reach my goals, and it is certainly not possible to be in a relationship with someone who starts everything with "my friends say... and therefore..."; because "eagles fly alone but sheep flock together" (Polish Proverb).

What is the Real Source of Any Disagreement?

People create disagreements as much as they attract them. And if a person believes that you can't be successful, that person is already manifesting a predisposition to attract a disagreement that will lead to a forceful transition.

The more you push yourself towards success, the faster this will occur. You never change as much as others do. When your beliefs conflict with theirs, one must change or the relationship must end. This is why it is so hard to share a life with someone who doesn't possess the same visions and faith as you do, someone who is, fundamentally, blind.

Most people only see a portion of your soul, and as you keep expanding, they may refuse the portions that don't match their expectations. This resentment is what causes ruptures whenever we are moving towards our goals. And the faster we change, the more we should accept such situations as inevitable.

In a world of donkeys, horses run alone. You can't expect chickens to fly with you, as you transit from being a chicken into becoming an eagle.

Many Hollywood movies lead us to believe in the lie that two persons can be completely different and yet be happy together, and I wish this was true, but too many painful experiences have shown me otherwise. The stupid insult the wise; those who fail betray those who don't; the poor resent the rich; the sick insult the healthy; the atheists put the patience of the most spiritual to the test.

You can't change these dynamics, and that is the saddest part of the law of attraction. As you work on yourself to become wealthier, everyone in your life who opposes it, who is jealous, who is resentful of your success, will remove their mask and show their true face to you, and surprise you with their real self, beneath the one they made you believe for too long.

You can't get more from life without sacrificing a lot. That is the painful part of this law. But I have done it many times. I have sacrificed many people to this law. And I must say, God sacrificed them and me along the process too, and as much as I did, because that is the law of this world.

The law of attraction is not some wishful thinking that allows you to get what you want without a price, but the mother of all laws. If you want more, you have to grow bigger than your pain, because you can't grow without leaving behind your old self and everything that made it be so.

The Law of Attraction in a Nutshell

Among all the religions that I studied, I found that the earliest contain the most profound truths on the law of attraction. Anyone who studies such scriptures, will understand a lot when compared to reading recent bestsellers, even though the language may be more allegoric and filled with symbolism.

Another thing that I need to say, as it is often neglected, is that karma and love set the rules for any of our methods. I personally know that my life is about to change, when I am losing people I love, friends I want to keep, or when being forced out of where I want to stay. Because this law does not forgive and is not blind.

As I am also experienced in occultism, I was able to understand why it works like this. If the people we know are against our dreams, either we lose the dreams or we lose them. You can't avoid quarrels and insults that others will create in order to justify an unavoidable transition.

This is why the majority of humanity is actually asleep, as this sleep comes in the form of unawareness, a complete unconsciousness to the mechanics of the world, operating around them and also inside of them. Basically speaking, the vast majority of the people operate by default, as effects of the spiritual mechanics in their reality. And because of this, they tend to pay a heavier price for their karma. The less they understand these principles, the more painful can be the influence of karma on them.

A few days ago, for example, a friend invited me out and then, after speaking compulsively, she started crying, and saying that she has no friends and spends her weekends crying in bed because she feels lonely and nobody wants to spend time with her. And I could feel sympathetic towards her, except that she cheated on her boyfriend, and invested her time on the wrong people, simply because they would go out with her to bars and clubs, and support her need to get drunk on the weekends, while the boyfriend wouldn't.

After being used as much as she used her friends, they moved on with their life and never again felt the need to talk to her. After insulting her boyfriend because of her selfish needs, she lost him too. And now, she is paying for what she did. This is karma but a karma that she herself created.

The law of attraction is the law of cause and effect, also known as karma. It can be positive or negative, because you attract what you do, and you do according to what you think, which is a reflection of what you believe. If your beliefs are wrong, you attract suffering; if your beliefs are right, you attract happiness. In a resume...

- If you think that love is a commodity, you attract loneliness;

- If you believe that friendships are meant to satisfy egotism, you attract betrayal;

- If you prioritize friendships above relationships, you attract abandonment;

- If you push away those who love you, you attract despair;

- If you value short term pleasures, you attract suffering.

How much loneliness and suffering one has to endure in order to understand these things? She couldn't understand and became angry when I said that she would have to experience loneliness for a longer period of time, possibly even a whole year, to see why her life was like that. When she asked me why, I tried to explain, but she kept demanding a shorter answer, so I gave her the shortest answer possible: "You are too stupid."

Why Affirmations aren't Enough to Create Changes?

I have used affirmations in the past to be able to shift my life into what is now, but found myself blocked recently, and then losing money, and that's when I came to the conclusion that affirmations aren't enough, at least for me. I also started doing many courses on wealth, to see if I could make more by correcting the strategies I was using, and nothing worked as well. Meanwhile, I realized that everyone that gets my knowledge, always attracts much more money than I do. And that, because my subconscious mind is more heavy than theirs.

I kept trying many more techniques, to improve my results, namely, self-hypnosis and meditation, but now my approach is different, as I realized how many popular techniques can end up working against us. Besides, there are many outside elements beyond our control that affect us too. Not many people understand this, because of how we were led to perceive the world and human behavior in the latest hundred years, but, you see, psychology is not really psychology, but more like a science about observable behaviors or "behaviorology", for it focuses on observations and not mechanics, analyzes instincts and changes, but not human upgrades in consciousness or awareness. And, likewise, religion is not really religion, but a compilation of cult-worshipping dogmas, that most followers agree upon, but don't fully understand and don't want to understand either, on the premise that such higher understanding may exclude them from the herd mentality they are familiar with.

The complexity of the world is beyond the reach of most minds, for they are not prepared for that level of reality. They are immersed in it but can't really perceive it. And that's where I appear, for my responsibility as an author is to upgrade the state of humanity to a higher vibration.

In other words, if I want help others, I have to be the one helping myself, for I won't find anyone with more to offer me, and I am always wasting my time when trying to find such people. Not many people really understand how the mind, the spirit and life itself operate altogether, or how they are interconnected, to shape our ever eternal personality. And this, probably, because they themselves get deceived by their own thoughts. And yet, there are many scientific studies showing us what I am referring to, for it has been proven, times enough, that our reality is ever adapting to our thoughts as much as our thoughts shape this same reality.

It could seem like a simplistic approach, looking at the world from this angle, but only if you disregard the fact that everyone on the planet is connected at a subconscious level, which is the same as to say that, the thoughts of everyone you interact with affect your own.

Now, when you compare affirmations, hypnosis, knowledge and therapy, with what I just said, you realize that you are competing with a subconscious mind that is, to a vast extent, beyond your control. That's why we fail systematically, despite our conscious efforts. And this is also why, whatsoever you wish to do, will never remove your money blocks, as they are not really yours to begin with. The only way to solve this problem consists in addressing the mechanics of the spiritual universe.

The evidence of the efficiency of this method will turn out to be very obvious to you as soon as you apply it. Because by working on yourself, on a spiritual and mental level, your reality, and everyone that is within it, will shift, as if controlled by an external force beyond their awareness. And this, because it is indeed how reality operates.

We are all connected by an invisible net, and as you reorganize your place mentally within this net, you will see the outside words shifting too, in order to match it. And because of what I just explained, the process is much faster than what you would get by using affirmations. Without a proper understanding of the mechanics of the spiritual world, affirmations can, very often, only increase your state of anxiety towards money, but not do much for your outcome.

Your Emotional Relationship With Money

Money is a currency in which a value is exchanged by another value. It can be gold, dollars, books, clothes, or anything else, including knowledge in any shape or form.

Many people apply this type of transaction when exchanging their time for money, for example. They are saying that 160 monthly hours of their life and 1,920 hours of each of their years, is equivalent to a salary that pays for their rent and food, and barely more than that. And that's a very poor agreement on which many billions of humans rely upon and agree with, as if saying that they have very low market value.

Once that happens, keeping people alive becomes a luxury rather than a necessity.

In other words, money in itself is not real, but merely the method we use to exchange value. If you buy a jacket that costs you a month's salary, then you worked a whole month for that jacket. And that is why, when people dress fine clothes, and feel wealthy, they also feel good about themselves, with a higher perception of themselves and a higher self-worth; they smile more, walk straight and experience life from the standpoint of holding to more confidence and abundance.

This mental state of relaxation makes people feel good about their existence, as if overcompensating for their lack of self-worth with material acquisitions. And the less spiritual values they have, the more they will feel this way.

Now, let us invert all that, and you will come to the conclusion that certain emotions and attitudes are related to wealth, while others are not. It is difficult to feel confident when you can barely make it to the end of the month with your expenses. This doesn't mean that your attitude and emotions will be enough to attract wealth, but rather that they are an expression of your self-worth, your subconscious beliefs, which, on the other hand, are based on what you consider to deserve. And that's where you find the reasons to why you've attracted a certain amount to your life, and no more or less than that.

You are manifesting what you consider to be your self-worth — your value as a human being — in your decisions, actions and, as a consequence, the amount of money you attract towards yourself too.

If you can make yourself feel worthy and rich, you're already halfway to your results. But only if you understand why you were not feeling like that before; i.e., if you realize what you need in your life to transform your emotions in that direction.

Maybe there is someone invalidating your social worth, maybe someone told you that you deserve less than what you have or not even that, maybe you tell yourself every day that you don't deserve more. Whatsoever is the reason, it is built into your daily habits and thoughts. As soon as you start perceiving yourself as more valuable, you will seek for more valuable jobs, where you get more respect and pay, you will seek for better business ideas, and you will basically produce more value to the world.

As your self-worth increases, so does the value of what you give back to humanity, which in return brings back more value to your life by this same exchange principle.

It is only when you start resenting life because of those who hurt you, that you shutdown your magnetic ability to attract more self-worth, and in the process, also more money.

Why are Money and Social Status Interrelated?

The reason why most people put so much importance in their appearance and reputation, is because they instinctively perceive these things as related to their survival, their status, their own worth, and as a result, what they can get in value from others.

This was an efficient way to climb the social ladder in the past, and even become a monarch. But it is not anymore a perspective so worthy as a direct path as it was before. Today, your value can be built in many other ways, even though it is fundamentally rooted in how you see yourself, and not how other see you. The more valuable you consider yourself to be, the more value you possess and attract. The challenge is in being able to do this while feeling contempt from others.

Now, obviously, as with people, objects assume a different value depending on where you present them. And that's why money is more valuable than any other object, as the value is the same everywhere in the world. The amount, on the other hand, of such value, is relative, if we consider it from the viewpoint of its usage, for in the phillipines $200 is a months' salary, while in the US it is barely enough for anything more than groceries. So, as you can see, how much you need depends on many factors. Any value is relative to the context in which it is applied.

The same can be said about your personal value, as your skills are more valuable in some parts of the world than others. Even your appearance can be perceived as more attractive in some parts of the planet but not in others. Why do we, for example, value white people so much nowadays? Because they appear in movies. Their value has been upgraded, in the form of superheroes, romantic actors, and so on. If those same white people were often portrayed as terrorists and petty criminals, their value would decrease. And yet, the value of a skin color is being upgraded or downgraded by trends. This is why you will get more love in some parts of the world than others, depending on how you appear to the locals.

The same applies to your services, goods, and many other components of your individuality as a human being.

As most people want to believe in an idealistic world, in which everyone is perceived as equal, they fail to adjust themselves to their surroundings, and in doing so, can't understand why they are being devalued or how they could increase their results by continuing in being themselves.

In order to illustrate this with a personal example, I can tell you that in most European states nobody believes I make a living as an author. Because most Europeans don't read, don't value reading, and assume that books have no value. And I can't make them believe in something they don't value. Therefore, my own value as a person, decreases.

They don't consider me important as a human being. And that's why few people in Europe care about spending time with me, which, as a result, makes me experience a more lonely life, in all aspects, including in my love life. European women are definitely not attracted to authors, because in Europe being an author has been associated with lack of wealth, insanity and loneliness.

On the other hand, if I am in the United States or China, everything changes within days, and I barely have time for myself. As soon as people know that I am an author, they want to invite me out, spend time with me, and talk to me about all kind of things; and even women are genuinely more interested in a potential relationship with me too. Again, the same appearance, but with a completely different perceived value, leads me to a completely different life experience too, in what regards perceived social value, relationships and even the potential to form connections that will literally guide me towards an increase of my wealth and improvements on my social circle.

This differentiation is so rooted in the culture, that nearly all Europeans I encounter, whenever they want to read books, typically select what was written by North American authors. Not only they devalue their own authors but also value more North American authors by default. And yet, if any of those North American authors were living in Europe, they would not be perceived as valuable.

It is certainly ridiculous when my friends refuse to buy my books because I live in Europe but choose to buy a book with less content than mine, published by an author living in the United States, while knowing that such author is selling less copies than me and has a lower rank than mine; but that's the power of social status over wealth.

Why Certain Cultural Values Can Keep You Poor?

As I can make money online, I can experience a dual lifestyle, in which I am perceived as a loser in Europe, while making more money sleeping than those who treat me like a rat. On the other hand, and as a result of that incongruence, my self-esteem is diminished, and so is my income.

Now, whenever I am traveling in countries where I am more respected, my books become better due to my clarity of mind, and more interesting too; I get better ideas for better books, and I also attract more money. And I guarantee you, I have seen this too often to call it a coincidence. As a matter of fact, I did not realize how connected my emotions and my income were, until I realized that I am constantly angry in Europe. My anger is a result of my personal worth being constantly under attack, with insults, and boring conversations that intend to reflect other's self doubts on me. They will ask things like, "How is it possible to make money with books?", "Do you only sell books?", "Anyone buys those books?", or "Who wants your books?"

I have never ever had to answer those stupid questions anywhere else but only in Europe. However, the questions rewire my brain, as if someone was telling me, "Don't think you should be making so much money". It is another way of also saying, "You don't deserve what you have".

If I tell you not to think about a pink elephant, that's exactly what you will be thinking about. And that's why the stupidity of others constantly affects your own concept of self-worth, either you like it or not.

It is because of that, that I started losing more than 80% of what I was earning before; which led me to study the topic I am showing you now and the conclusions of such self-analysis. This book is far much more important to me than it is for anyone else reading it. I built it to protect my mind from such vicious and constant attacks on my self-esteem through both indirect and direct invalidation.

The only thing that I can't answer you at the moment, despite the vast amount of knowledge I possess today, is if you can be in a relationship with a poor person while being rich. Sadly, so far, I am forced to tell you that this isn't possible. A poor person has a poor mindset, and will constantly push your finances downwards by default. I am yet to experience otherwise, including in the cases of women who go from rag to riches, or those who simply come from very poor households and today live independently with well-paid jobs.

Why Your Friends Can Keep You Poor?

Whenever your self-perceived value, whatsoever is the cause of it, is inferior to your exterior value, you tend to work more for less in return. This is why the scarcity of jobs available forces workers to accept lower salaries. But whenever your self-perceived value is superior to your exterior value, you overrate yourself, and end up alone, perceived as arrogant, an outcast, a rebel, and a crazy person. In fact, that's quite often the main cause behind candidates being excluded after their job interviews.

That attitude, in return, will affect your personal value too. As a result, if you want to increase your sense of worth and also your income, you need to create a balance between the inside and the outside; and you can only accomplish this through your emotions, and the constant maintenance of a superior state of mind, which, if accepted by the outside world, and can be maintained by habit. If failing to do so, you need a constant exercising of a fabricated projection. This is why people are constantly faking their social image, and living in fear of what others think.

In other words, the less value others see in you, the more inner work you need to do with yourself, though the application of this book, and using visualizations and affirmations. You always need to do more than what is normal, to maintain or increase your state of living, because, by default, society will stop you from changing towards the outside of the role that has been labeled for you inside that same society.

This is simply how most people perceive themselves and how this world has always been organized. A fish can't become an eagle, even though a human being can be prey or preyer, slave or owner, of his own fate. And yet, most people don't look at reality from this standpoint. They consider their own nature to be immutable, as the nature of any other animal.

Paradoxically, the more anybody considers himself to be just a social animal, the more he or she will be prone to believe in the immutable nature of his own soul. This is why you shouldn't want to hang out with either Darwinists or Atheists.

The Big Lie in Equalitarianism

As most people are jealous of the living standards of some and even resent it, we are often fed with lies in what regards the idealization of the world, being socialism and communist the most prominent weapons. But let us not be fooled, for "when a whole society demands a high standard of living and yet doesn't concentrate on the personal production of valuable products, it is finished" (L. Ron Hubbard).

The truth is that, whenever people have a low self-esteem, a low self-worth, and low expectations, their production levels reflects that, for they are slow, lazy, ignorant, and in their arrogance, don't feel the need to learn or improve, or work more hours. And that is why procrastination and laziness are diseases of the mind related to a low self-worth.

One can't attract wealth, unless he is reflecting the same worth he intends to get, through his own personality and actions. We always need to produce much more value in whatever we do, or the confidence we transmit to others, than what we get in return, because, simply putting it, not everyone who loves you, will buy from you, and not everything you do, even if of high quality, will be perceived as high quality for everyone else.

In my case, for example, this reflects in my constant improvement in editing books, changing covers, and delivering more content professionally. As my own perception of my value increases, my works' value also increases, and as a result I get more wealth.

If I expected others to give me that higher value for no other reason, I would be waiting for my own death, because people always perceive us with much less value than the one we already have.

This phenomenon can be seen on a wider scale, for "in a society led astray by crackpot economics,... the rich (most of whom work like mad) are seen as idle or even criminals; the best of way of life is made to appear to be idleness; one seems to be owed a living without any effort on his own part" (L. Ron Hubbard). This type of sickness formed under an ignorant mindset towards money leads many people to believe in what is called equalitarianism. "It declares that everyone should get the same pay and have the same standard of living. It does not mention that anyone should do any work. It holds that the better worker should not be better rewarded. It would crash any society" (L. Ron Hubbard).

Whenever you apply social falsehoods to your own life, you are doomed to fail. This is why it is equally important to understand how money works, how wealth is made, as it is to put efforts in the accumulation of more, because, fundamentally, you are dealing with a bridge between yourself and the rest of the world — your identity and how the world perceives it. You can't attract more and keep it without understanding that same world and how it views you and your unique value.

In order to attract more abundance to your life, you need to work on yourself. You change your reality and your outcome by changing yourself, and what has been preventing you from reaching your best.

Step 1: Deprogramming Your Mind

The following list of questions intends to bring forth the memories holding you back —hidden from your awareness and inside your subconscious mind — to the surface.

It may seem difficult to answer most of these questions at first, but you should repeat the experience as much as possible, in order to keep awakening more and more memories from your past. The more you use this system, the more your subconscious mind will be clean from all money blocks, the more powerful will be your magnetism to attract wealth and, most importantly, the less impactful the thoughts and words of others in what regards money will be on you.

Every time you can't answer one question, simply move to the following one. Repeat this list every single morning, when your brain is relaxed and well aware, as it is much harder to do this exercise when you are exhausted from a full day of work.

Always try to obtain the earliest memory you can, or the most recent, when you can't remember most of your past. Also, whenever succeeding in this process of remembering, try to recall how old you were in each memory that you bring to the surface.

You will see that, the more you repeat this list, the better your overall memory and focus will become, and the happier you will feel.

Many other events in your social life will manifest accordingly as well, in order to match the transformations that you feel within yourself by using this list.

This said, let us begin with the cleaning of your subconscious mind. Please recall a time when...

1. A person much smaller than you resented your size.
2. A person bigger than you made you feel inferior.
3. A person would not let you start something.
4. A person would not let you finish something.

5. You found a space too small.
6. You found a space too big.
7. You were pushed back because you were too small.
8. You were pushed back because you were too big.
9. You were rejected by a team.
10. You were chosen by a team.
11. You found somebody had lied about how bad you were.
12. You found somebody had lied about how good you were.
13. You discovered you had been right, after all.
14. You found your decision would have been best.
15. You solved a problem nobody else could.
16. You found you could ignore somebody's opinion.
17. Someone praised your results.
18. You won a competition.
19. You were admired by your looks.
20. You controlled a machine.
21. A machine controlled you.
22. You accomplished a difficult journey.
23. You discovered your competence.
24. You discovered your limitations.
25. An enemy begged for mercy.
26. Someone begged for forgiveness.
27. Someone cried because of you.
28. You cried because of someone.
29. Someone hurt you physically.
30. You hurt someone physically.
31. You drew blood from somebody else.
32. You were able to get away from somebody who invalidated you.
33. You discovered you were right and one of your parents was wrong.
34. You found you could get better.
35. You surpassed the expectations of others.
36. You did something that somebody considered impossible.
37. You surprised yourself with your own endurance.
38. You discovered you could understand a difficult subject.
39. You did a job nobody believed possible.

Step 2: Removing Money Blocks

We will now follow with another exercise, by erasing your sense of unworthiness in what regards being wealthy. Please recall a time when...

1. A person much smaller than you resented you for owning something.
2. A person bigger than you resented you for owning something.
3. A person would't let you start something that was profitable for you.
4. An object was too expensive for you but you bough it.
5. You were threatened because you looked rich.
6. You were chosen by a team because you seemed confident.
7. You found you were adequate to make money from work.
8. You found you were inadequate for a job but got paid anyway.
9. You found somebody was wrong about how bad you were at making money.
10. You found somebody was right about how good you were at making money.
11. You discovered you had been right, after all about how to make money.
12. You found your decision would have been best to increase profits.
13. You found a solution nobody else could and made money with it.
14. You found you could ignore somebody's opinion about money.
15. You found you couldn't ignore somebody's opinion about money.
16. Your skills were admired and were paid well.
17. You won a competition and received a valuable award.
18. You found you could work more than most people.
19. You made money online.
20. You made money illegally.
21. You made money using your brain.
22. You made money using your heart.
23. You made money using your hands.
24. You made money using your intuition.
25. You made money using your luck.
26. You accomplished a difficult plan to increase profits.
27. You discovered your competence in making money.

28. Someone you disliked begged you for money.
29. Someone you liked begged you for money.
30. Someone cried because you got something valuable.
31. Someone hurt you physically because of money.
32. Someone hurt you emotionally because of money.
33. You hurt someone physically because of money.
34. You hurt someone emotionally because of money.
35. You were able to get away from somebody who invalidated your potential to make money.
36. You discovered you were right and one of your parents was wrong in what regards your potential to make money.
37. You found you could get better at profiting with an activity.
38. You were afraid to fail but didn't and got money at the end.
39. You surpassed the expectations of others in creating profit.
40. You disappointed someone because you became successful.
41. You disappointed someone because you earned a good salary.
42. You disappointed someone because you were dressing expensive clothes.
43. You disappointed someone because you were enjoying your money to travel.
44. You made money with something that others considered impossible.
45. You surprised yourself with your own endurance in working for money.
46. You surprised yourself with your own ideas on how to make money.
47. You discovered you could understand how to make more money.
48. You did well in a profitable job when nobody believed it would be possible.
49. You were told that you would never be better than others.
50. Your mother made you feel inferior to someone else.
51. Your father made you feel inferior to someone else.
52. You were told that you would never be wealthy.
53. You ignored someone because he was poor.
54. You ignored someone because he was rich.
55. You were ignored by someone because you were poor.
56. You were ignored by someone because you were rich.

57. You had too much money in your wallet.
58. You had to be polite to someone who was wealthier than you.
59. Someone was polite to you because you looked wealthier.
60. Your clothes made you look rich.
61. You starved because you did not have enough money.
62. You found you didn't have to starve because you had enough money.
63. The vehicle where you were sitting made you look wealthy.
64. A space was too big for you and made you feel rich.
65. A table was big and full of abundance.
66. You could afford an expensive bill at the doctor or dentist.
67. Somebody made you feel rich because of your personality.
68. Somebody made you feel rich because of your background.
69. Somebody made you feel rich because of your family.
70. You held hands with someone rich.
71. You stripped someone rich.
72. You kissed a rich person.
73. You had sex with a rich person.
74. A person would't let you sell something.
75. You were rejected by a team because you were ambitious.
76. You were chosen by a team because you were ambitious.
77. Someone rich asked for your opinion.
78. Someone rich depended on you.
79. You found you were adequate for being better than others.
80. You found you were inadequate for being better than others.
81. You found somebody underestimated your potential.
82. You found somebody underestimated your intelligence.
83. You found somebody underestimated your experience.
84. You found your advice helped somebody make money.
85. You found your advice helped somebody have a better life.
86. You found you could make a child laugh with gifts you paid.
87. You found your decision saved you from poverty.
88. You found your decision attracted luck to your life.
89. You got lucky and you acted on it.
90. Someone gave you an opportunity and you took it.
91. You solved a problem nobody could help you with.

92. Your knowledge helped you make more money.
93. You made more money by investing with money.
94. Someone offered you money.
95. Someone borrowed you money.
96. You offered money to someone.
97. You borrowed money to someone.
98. Someone transferred money to your bank account.
99. You transferred money to someone's bank account.
100. Your own plans attracted luck towards your life.
101. Your own plans attracted luck towards someone else's life.
102. You discovered your competence in learning about money.
103. You discovered your competence in succeeding with a business.
104. You got money without asking for it.
105. Someone offered you holidays.
106. Someone offered you a bed to sleep.
107. Someone offered you a house to live.
108. Someone offered you a job you didn't ask for.
109. Someone invited you for dinner and paid.
110. Someone invited you for lunch and paid.
111. Someone invited you for a drink and paid.
112. You had lunch with someone wealthy.
113. You had dinner with someone wealthy.
114. You enjoyed a buffet in an expensive hotel.
115. You found you could get a better job.
116. You found you were the best in a job.
117. You made more money than you needed.
118. You made more money than you expected.
119. You found more money in your bank account than expected.
120. You made money doing something with passion.
121. You were happy with the amount of money received.
122. You made money easily and effortlessly.
123. You discovered how to make people want to pay you.
124. You were happy with having money.
125. You had just finished creating something that got you paid.
126. You felt energetic because you had money.

127. You felt free because you had money.
128. You felt strong because you had money.
129. You felt confident because you had money.
130. You felt safe because you had money.
131. Somebody was waiting for you to give you money.
132. You went somewhere to get paid.
133. You bought something you liked because someone offered you money.
134. You enjoyed a lifestyle in which you didn't have to worry about money.
135. You played a game with money.
136. Somebody thought you were important because you had money.
137. Somebody helped you get more money.
138. Somebody loved you because you looked wealthy.
139. You enjoyed the company of someone who was wealthy.
140. You made progress towards acquiring more money.
141. You walked with confidence because you felt wealthy.
142. You helped someone by giving him/her money.
143. You used money to bring to you someone you liked.
144. You used money to send away someone you disliked.
145. You lived well and at peace because of your wealth.
146. You were respected because of your wealth.
147. You got paid much earlier than expected.
148. Somebody rich lived too long.
149. Somebody rich was kind.
150. Somebody rich was friendly.
151. Somebody rich was honest.
152. Somebody rich lived with good health.
153. You saw something expensive and desirable and got it.
154. People looked at you and believed you were wealthy.
155. You earned money doing something that was easy for you.
156. You earned money doing something that was difficult for you.
157. You earned money doing something that you were qualified to do.
158. You earned money doing something that you weren't qualified to do.
159. You heard a pleasant voice talking about wealth.
160. You heard water running in a wealthy house.
161. You felt the heat from a fireplace in a wealthy house.

162. You heard the wind while in a wealthy house.
163. You heard a door opening in a wealthy house.
164. Someone wealthy admired you.
165. You heard a rich child laughing.
166. You met a good and rich person.
167. You met a happy and rich person.
168. You won money by being antagonistic.
169. You won money by being friendlier.
170. You admired something a rich person had.
171. You attacked someone successfully and got lucky.
172. A rich person depended on you to succeed.
173. A company depended on you to succeed.
174. Someone you admired offered you money.
175. You expected money and got it.
176. You refused money but got it anyway.
177. You were "attached" to something worthy.
178. You felt energetic while working for money.
179. You felt confident with how much money you made.
180. A city made you feel rich.
181. A city made you feel poor.
182. You influenced somebody to make more money.
183. You prevented someone from losing money.
184. You helped a poor person become rich.
185. You prevented a company from losing money.
186. You produced something of value to someone.
187. You were glad to avoid a quarrel about money.
188. You enjoyed the silence while feeling abundance.
189. You enjoyed the sound of birds singing while feeling wealthy.
190. You enjoyed loneliness while working for money.
191. You got to go to bed feeling you had created enough wealth.
192. You found it was a beautiful day and you had plenty of money.
193. You refused to work because you had enough money.
194. You surprised somebody by getting wealthier.
195. You contributed with your money to something.
196. You finally got rid of something wasting your money.

197. You finally got rid of someone wasting your money.
198. You stopped somebody from being stolen.
199. You stopped somebody from losing money.
200. Somebody understood your ideas to increase wealth.
201. You felt energetic with more money.
202. You produced something of value.
203. You harnessed some energy to make more money.
204. You were glad to be with a friend who was wealthy.
205. You realized your luck was good and you could attract money.
206. You overcame antagonism and made more money because of it.
207. You could tell the difference between a good and a bad idea.
208. A relative was proud of you for making more money.
209. Somebody was faithful to you and helped you get rich.
210. You received a pleasant call offering you money.
211. You found you had influence in increasing profits.
212. You were ambitious and made money because of it.
213. Many were proud of your achievements.
214. You were admired for your ability to make money.
215. You helped a company increase profits.
216. You helped a business owner make more money.
217. You kept a secret about making money.
218. Someone believed in your capacity to make money.
219. You understood how to get more money.
220. Someone appreciated your capacity to make good decisions.
221. Someone needed you because of money.
222. You were invited because of your experience with success.
223. You found yourself necessary in helping increase profits.
224. You won a struggle and made money because of it.
225. You were believed and got money because of it.
226. You rescued somebody from poverty.
227. Somebody was glad you were there to help save the company.
228. You conquered sorrow and made more money.
229. You conquered apathy and made more money.
230. You conquered depression and made more money.
231. You conquered resentment and anger and made more money.

232. You conquered chaos and confusion and made more money.
233. You were rewarded with more money.
234. They discovered you were valuable.
235. You were no longer unhappy because you got wealthier.
236. You got to go from somewhere to make more money.
237. You got a better job offer from another city/country and took it.
238. You were glad to shake hands with business owners.
239. You were true to your purpose and made more money.
240. You followed your dreams and got what you wanted.
241. You had plenty of time to make money.
242. You found out you weren't lazy in making money.
243. They discovered you weren't ignorant about money.
244. You did the impossible and got more money.
245. You didn't have to worry about income at the end of the month.
246. You had a good house because you had money to pay for it.
247. You discovered making money was easy.
248. They had confidence in your capacity to attract wealth.
249. They admitted you were clever at creating wealth.
250. You discovered you didn't have to worry about money.
251. Hope paid off and you got more money.
252. Your faith in your plan resulted in more money.
253. They did not believe you would succeed but you did.
254. You stood very straight because you felt wealthy.
255. You ate a good and expensive meal because you could afford it.
256. You were enjoying making money.
257. You were relaxed while working for money.
258. Your hands did something profitable.
259. You knew you looked good because you appeared wealthy.
260. You were running with the feeling of being wealthy.
261. You were walking and feeling wealthy.
262. You enjoyed traveling because you had money to spend.
263. You enjoyed standing still because you felt wealthy.
264. You enjoyed vacations in an expensive city because you could afford it.
265. You enjoyed vacations at the beach while feeling wealthy.
266. You handled a complicated purpose successfully and earned money.

267. You packed knowing that you had plenty of money in your bank account.
268. You enjoyed the morning because you felt wealthy.
269. You danced because you felt wealthy.
270. You enjoyed the night because you felt wealthy.
271. You enjoyed other people's company because you felt wealthy.
272. You felt smart because you were wealthy.
273. You amused people because you felt happy with wealth.
274. Someone wanted to spend time with you because you appeared rich.
275. You enjoyed seeing rain come down because you felt wealthy.
276. You made someone happy because you had money.
277. You prayed for a certain amount of money and got it.
278. You prayed for a certain lifestyle and got it.
279. Somebody you didn't like walked away from you because he/she resented your success.
280. Somebody you liked entered your life because you were successful.
281. You enjoyed just sitting and feeling wealthy.
282. You enjoyed a view because you felt wealthy.
283. You drove a good car and felt wealthy doing it.
284. You were happy for being richer than others.
285. You wanted to stay and did because you had money.
286. You wanted to leave and did because you had money.
287. You acquired something expensive you wanted.
288. You were proud to have something expensive.
289. Someone who wanted you poor moved away from you.
290. Someone who believed you would never be rich abandoned your life.
291. You maintained somebody in your life by using money.
292. You controlled somebody because you had money.
293. You paid someone for services to you.
294. You made profit from the work of someone else.
295. You escaped from a dangerous space because you had money.
296. You happily defied directions you had been given and made more money because of it.
297. You found somebody you wanted because you had money.
298. You acquired money you were not supposed to have and kept it.

299. You went back to something you had been pulled away from to profit.
300. You were right in disobeying someone and got richer because of it.
301. You read a forbidden book and got richer.
302. You found a profitable idea which had been hidden from you.
303. You were right and they were wrong about money.
304. You bullied somebody into giving you money.
305. You discovered you didn't necessarily have to go to sleep at night and could continue working.
306. You found money you didn't know was there.
307. You and a person you liked engaged in a profitable action.
308. A richer person you liked aided you.
309. You were glad to be alone making money.
310. Somebody aided your ambition to be wealthier.
311. You were among people who were richer than you.
312. A rich person entertained you and amused you.
313. You finally didn't have to be anxious about making money.
314. You found out you didn't have to be ashamed about your wealth.
315. Somebody you liked gave you money.
316. You were attractive to somebody richer than you.
317. You began a friendship with someone rich.
318. You liked somebody who was black and wealthy.
319. You liked somebody who was white and wealthy.
320. You liked somebody who was Latino and wealthy.
321. You liked somebody who was Arabic and wealthy.
322. Nobody could bother you while you were busy making money.
323. You had reached the bottom and started making money again.
324. You brought somebody an expensive present.
325. Somebody helped you build something that made you richer.
326. Somebody kissed you because you were wealthy.
327. You answered a call that intended to give you money.
328. You received a message about money you earned.
329. You enjoyed being careless about money.
330. You applied spiritual knowledge to finances and succeeded.
331. Somebody believed you were clever at making money.
332. You were comfortable with a rich person.

333. People had confidence in your capacity to get richer.
334. People realized you had courage to make money.
335. You created a group of wealthy people.
336. Your desire for wealth was answered.
337. You departed from a person who didn't want you to succeed.
338. An enemy to your successful lifestyle departed from you.
339. You drove an enemy of your wealth into despair.
340. Your determination won and you got wealthier.
341. You could tell the difference between poverty and wealth.
342. You found you were right to distrust somebody on money issues.
343. You had no doubt of someone's intention to make you richer.
344. You had no doubt of someone's intention to make you poorer.
345. Your effort was rewarded with more money.
346. You successfully encouraged somebody to be richer.
347. You put an end to a life of scarcity and poverty.
348. You knew you'd had enough wealth and took action.
349. You were equal to anyone who was wealthy.
350. You discovered you didn't have to be afraid of being rich anymore.
351. You fed somebody because you had money to help.
352. You fed animals because you had money to spend.
353. You discovered your enemies were poor.
354. People you loved hurt you because of jealousy.
355. People you trusted hurt you because of jealousy.
356. You used force on a rich person successfully.
357. You realized you were free from money worries.
358. You realized you were free from needing a job.
359. People found you generous with your money.
360. People made you happy for being rich.
361. You paid for a seminar to learn how to make money.
362. You were discovered to be interesting on your explanations about money.
363. You made somebody happy with something you sold them.
364. Somebody got richer with something you told them.
365. You found you could have love and money at the same time.
366. You found you could be wealthy and healthy at the same time.

367. Your luck in attracting money was excellent.
368. You decided not to marry because that person would make you poorer.
369. You gave somebody you liked an expensive gift.
370. You prevented somebody from losing money.
371. They discovered you could make money.
372. Somebody was proud of your capacity to attract money.
373. You discovered your regrets about money were in vain.
374. Somebody said you resembled someone rich.
375. You succeeded in creating wealth in spite of people's opinion.
376. Your search was rewarded with more wealth.
377. You found shame about your wealth wasn't necessary.
378. Your anxiety about money was for nothing.
379. Your fears about money weren't necessary.
380. Your guilt about money was for nothing.
381. Somebody had to respect your rights of ownership.
382. You discovered the difference between "no" and "now" in what regards increasing profits.
383. You discovered the difference between "no" and "know" as in knowing, in what regards increasing profits.
384. They discovered how valuable you were.
385. You walked with somebody rich.
386. You had drinks with somebody rich.
387. Somebody admired something expensive you had.
388. Something aided you make more money.
389. You astonished people with something expensive.
390. You attacked something that threatened your finances successfully.
391. You attacked a business owner and got your money back.
392. You charmed somebody with wealth.
393. You became certain about your capacity to make more money.
394. You were happy to receive money you deserved.
395. You did something to get money which others considered too difficult.
396. You were excited by having more money.
397. You made money quickly.
398. You overcame the fear of being rich.

399. You were proud of your possessions.
400. You hurried to get money and achieved it.
401. You imagined a new way to make money and made it.
402. You dreamed about having more money and got it.
403. You watched money coming in.
404. You enjoyed watching your bank account growing.
405. You kissed your hand because you felt wealthy.
406. You threw money into the air because you felt rich.
407. You discovered the origin of money.
408. An object made you feel rich.
409. You were glad to receive money.
410. You took money to safety.
411. You convinced someone of the value of your work.
412. You were pleasantly alone working for money.
413. You were happy with the sunrise because you felt wealthy.
414. You had to give up a career to make more money.
415. You had to give up a hobby to make more money.
416. You had to give up a dream to make more money.
417. You had to give up a relationship to make more money.
418. Somebody you admired showed you how to make money.
419. Somebody you loved showed you how to make money.
420. Somebody made you take care of their money.
421. You were corrected about money "for your own good".
422. Somebody tried to stop you from making money but you kept on anyway.
423. You found other people weren't wiser than you about money.
424. Everybody thought you were wrong about money but discovered you had been right.
425. You were really enjoying yourself because you had plenty of money to spend.
426. You drew a plan to make more money and people followed it.
427. You watched a person you liked making more money.
428. You saw a person you disliked getting poorer.
429. You were classified as wealthy by a poor person.
430. You were classified as wealthy by a rich person.

Step 3: Increasing Your Magnetic Power

The purpose of this exercise is to increase the power of your magnetic mind to attract wealth. For we all have a certain magnetic strength. Even a beggar has one, operating at a very low frequency, related to his basic survival.

This magnetic field is composed of beliefs and emotions. And we can control our beliefs with education and a reprogramming of our thoughts, but we can hardly reprogram our emotions, and these are much more powerful, up to five thousand times more than our thoughts.

In order to accomplish this, we need to exercise our emotions as if we were going to the gym to train our body. Therefore, you must use this exercise as a mental gym for your capacity to feel good around money and wealth in general.

In regards to positive reinforcements, please recall a time when…

1. A wealthy person was having fun at making money.
2. An exciting activity was making people wealthy.
3. A millionaire was excited about his business.
4. Someone wealthy was beautiful.
5. Someone wealthy was well-dressed.
6. You saw a beautiful house owned by a wealthy person.
7. Someone was happy with a very profitable business.
8. Somebody was interested in a profitable idea.
9. Someone wealthy was interested in you.
10. Someone wealthy was in love with you.
11. Someone wealthy thought you were smart.
12. Someone wealthy thought you could help them make money.
13. Someone wealthy did something you like to do.
14. Someone wealthy agreed with you.
15. Someone wealthy copied you.
16. Someone wealthy asked for your opinion.
17. Someone wealthy followed you.
18. Someone wealthy depended on you.

19. Somebody rich thought you were compassionate.
20. Somebody rich thought you were caring.
21. Somebody rich thought you were good.
22. Somebody rich thought you were helpful.
23. Somebody rich thought you were responsible.
24. Somebody rich thought you were charismatic.
25. Somebody rich thought you were humble.
26. Somebody rich thought you were supporting others.
27. Somebody rich thought you were honest.
28. Somebody rich thought you were smart.
29. Somebody rich thought you were friendly.
30. Somebody rich thought you were polite.
31. Somebody rich thought you were mentally healthy.
32. Somebody rich thought you were joyful.
33. Somebody rich thought you made them feel safe.
34. Somebody rich thought you were deserving of much more.
35. Somebody rich thought you should be rich too.

Now, in regards to negative reinforcements, please recall a time when...

1. Someone poor wasn't interested in you.
2. Someone poor rejected a relationship with you.
3. Someone poor thought you couldn't help them make money.
4. Someone poor was disagreeing with you.
5. Someone poor was ignoring you.
6. Someone poor rejected your opinion.
7. Someone poor betrayed you.
8. Somebody poor thought you were selfish.
9. Somebody poor thought you were greedy.
10. Somebody poor thought you were evil.
11. Somebody poor thought you were manipulative.
12. Somebody poor thought you were controlling.
13. Somebody poor thought you were emotionally abusive.
14. Somebody poor thought you were arrogant.
15. Somebody poor thought you were cheating others.

16. Somebody poor thought you were stealing money.
17. Somebody poor thought you were a criminal.
18. Somebody poor thought you were a liar.
19. Somebody poor thought you were stupid.
20. Somebody poor thought you were unfriendly.
21. Somebody poor thought you were rude.
22. Somebody poor thought you were insane.
23. Somebody poor thought you were scary.
24. Somebody poor thought you were dangerous.
25. Somebody poor thought you were undeserving.

Step 4: Rehabilitating Your Imagination

Now that you answered the previous questions and became more aware of what is stopping you from becoming wealthy, we will proceed by rehabilitating your capacity in using your imagination to attract wealth.

Please recall a moment in your life, when...

- You foresaw how money should be made and arranged your life accordingly.
- You imagined yourself wealthy and worked towards it.
- You did a masterpiece of creation that gave you more money.
- You saw money come into actuality as you had imagined.
- You imagined money and attracted an opportunity to make it.
- Your vision was complemented with more wealth.
- You made profit out of your imagination.
- You noticed somebody making money in the same way as you do.
- You found somebody wealthy using a mannerism you used.
- You adopted a mannerism from a wealthy person.
- You made faces like a wealthy man/woman at yourself in the mirror.
- You decided to be completely different from a poor person.
- You decided to be similar to a rich person.

Now, close your eyes, and imagine yourself having a conversation with someone you know, in the future, and telling this person what you have done. The conversation must sound realistic to you and include all the things that you expect to achieve.

If you do this exercise correctly, you will likely find yourself in a *Déjà vu* situation with such individual, and describing the same after accomplishing it.

After you finish, repeat the same exercise with five different individuals from your life.

Step 5: Realigning Your Spirit

The following exercise intends to go deeper than the previous ones, this time by changing your whole future in this life and the next. The purpose here is to address your money issues at a spiritual level, by looking at different areas of your spiritual development. And you may recall memories from past lives when doing it, but don't worry about that, and simply proceed by working with the lists shown.

Level 1: The Scale of Human Emotions:

Please recall a time when...

- You felt in apathy because you had no money.
- You were crying due to lack of money.
- You were afraid to lose all your money.
- You were angry because someone took your money.
- You were against a group because they wanted your money.
- You were bored because you didn't have enough money to spend.
- You felt your salary was enough to pay rent and other expenses.
- You felt you deserved a higher salary.
- You were cheerful with how much money you were making.
- You were excited and proud to make more money than others.

Level 2: The Scale of Chakras:

Please recall a time when...

- Root Chakra: You made money because you were in the right city.

- Sacral Chakra: You made money because people were sexually attracted to you.

- Solar Plexus Chakra: You made money by being a leader.

- Heart Chakra: You received money because people loved you.

- Throat Chakra: You made money by speaking to others.

- Third Eye Chakra: You made money by being creative.

- Crown Chakra: You made money with an idea.

Level 3: The Scale of Personal Influence:

Please recall a time when...

- Self: You did something you wanted and earned money.

- Family: You helped your family get more money.

- Group: You helped your friends in becoming wealthier.

- Humanity: You helped a stranger.

- Nature: You gave food to animals.

- Planet: You helped the planet by recycling.

- Spirit: You improved yourself through a religious activity.

- God: You did something that you felt God wanted from you.

Step 6: Rewriting Your Karma

Quite often, the reason why we can't be rich, is because the people we love the most, or respect, or associate ourselves with, for any reason, don't want us to be wealthy, don't believe we can be wealthy, or simply don't trust our capacity to succeed, or don't believe we deserve it. And it is because we subconsciously fear the consequences of betraying their beliefs, that we end up sabotaging our results, especially if they are family members or someone we live with.

If you followed the previous exercises effectively, you should be able to answer the following questions. If you can't, just go back to the previous lists until this is possible. You will notice that, as you feel better with yourself, and more capable, identifying who is against your goals of becoming wealthier becomes easier too. Many of them, as explained previously, will start showing themselves by removing their mask in front of you, usually in the form of insults. That's when you realize, if you had any doubts before, what other people really think of you, and what is their hidden intention behind their words.

As truth becomes more evident, and as "money blockers" are removed or remove themselves, people who support your goals will also start manifesting themselves and wanting to spend more time with you. The inner and the outer worlds are related, so you don't really need to do an intensive research on the intentions of the ones who surround you. All you need to do is work on yourself with this book.

As you remove the mental blocks from yourself, those who are in your life — because their presence is justified by such subconscious beliefs and emotions — will vanish. And I am sorry to tell you, but if it is your wife, she may find someone else to cheat on you, she may sabotage the relationship and end the marriage, or she may actually die.

I've had girlfriends who, by trying to stop me while I was working on myself, created a huge damage in themselves. One of them applied on me magic spells — which she learned from her mother who works as a professional witch —

and those spells backfired on her, first by consuming the energy of her body, and making her look twenty years older than she was, in just a few months, and then by causing her to lose her job.

Another one, by trying to make me lose my money, while I was using the law of attraction to get more, got a cancer. And the last one, had to be operated by emergency after a cyst blew up in her body.

I have already told this last girl that she can die, if she insists in coming back to my life while trying to make me stop from reaching my goals. But because most people don't understand how life works, they commit suicide, when driving themselves against a wall of changes.

I do change extremely fast, because of the amount of knowledge I have on magic and the mind, but other people don't, because they lack such knowledge. So, when I am changing, they are often not prepared for it, and insist in stopping me in all ways they consider to be possible, ending up attracting more damage to themselves.

This is something which you will hardly be able to explain to someone. However, the more you apply these exercises, the more you will notice the life of those around you shifting to make yours easier. This said, let us proceed with the next questions.

List 1: Rewriting Your Karmic Identity:

In what rewards your thoughts about money, answer the following:

- Who you are most like? Who said so?
- Who used to be afraid of money?
- Who was never supposed to amount to anything?
- Who associated you with poor people too much?
- Who would you most want to be like? Why?
- Who would you most hate to be like? Why?

- Who held that you amounted to nothing?
- Who flattered you for being good at making money?
- Who helped you make money?
- Who said you would never be rich?
- Who said you couldn't be rich?
- Who said you should be poor?
- Who wanted you to remain poor?

List 2: Rewriting Your Emotions with Intention:

In what rewards your emotions about money, answer the following:

- When did you feel not supported? Why? How old were you?
- When did you feel you were poorer than others? Why? How old were you?
- When did you feel that you couldn't be rich? Why? How old were you?
- When did you feel that you would never be rich? Why? How old were you?

List 3: Rewriting Your Self-Worth:

It is common for those who have been raised by narcissistic parents to feel unworthy. They typically make us feel this way by using invalidation, disdain, disgust, contempt and envy.

In order to heal yourself from those programs, please recall a time when someone said or implied to you the following:

1. "I love you because you are my son/daughter but I don't like you as a person."

2. "I love you but I don't like what you do."
3. "I love you but I don't like how you think."
4. "I love you but you are too stupid."
5. "You are just like your father."
6. "You are just like your mother."
7. "You are just like... (now fill the blank with the name of someone hated).
8. "Other parents are luckier than we are."
9. "Other families are better than ours."

Now, recall a time when...

- You were told you were not enough.

- You were told you are not lovable.

- You were told that you don't deserve to be loved.

- You were told that you can't be loved.

- You were told that you are not normal.

- You were told that you are evil.

List 4: Eliminating Limiting Beliefs:

Now understand your limiting beliefs by completing the following sentences:

1. I can't have the money I want in my life because...
2. I can have the money I want because...
3. I can't be successful because...
4. I can be successful because...
5. I don't deserve to be successful because...
6. I deserve to be successful because...
7. I don't deserve to be a millionaire because...
8. I deserve to be a millionaire because...

List 5: Redefining Your Karmic Relationship with Money:

For this exercise, I want you to write a letter to money, as if it was your friend and lover. Talk about your emotions and feelings, based on what you learned about yourself doing all the previous exercises so far. Start with the following:

Dear Money, I ask you for forgiveness,...

List 6: Clarifying Your Relationship with God and Abundance:

Repeat the previous exercise by writing a letter to God.

When writing your letter, answer the following:

- Why do you want the money?
- How much money you want?
- How will you use the money you get?
- Why is such amount of money important to you?
- Why do you think you deserve it?
- How will you invest the money?
- How will you treat people if you're wealthier?
- How will you treat the poor if you have abundance?
- How will you fulfill your spiritual path by having more money?
- How will you handle your personality with more money?
- How will you confront your past when having more money?
- How will you face your fears if you have more money?
- How will you confront your enemies if you have more money?
- How will you talk to your family if you have more money?
- How will you find or accept love if you have more money?

- What kind of person you wish to be if you have more money?

- Where do you want to live if you're wealthy?

Begin your letter by writing the following:

Dear God, please send me more money because…

Step 7: Opening Quantum Gates

Now that you have removed the money blocks from your mind, by identifying which ones were against your success, it is time to expand the potential for more opportunities to succeed to manifest in your life.

Complete the following sentences and then close your eyes, and repeat the answers to yourself, by transforming such answers into mantras. While repeating them, visualize what you say in your mind. Because, doing this, will help you in shifting your vibration towards attracting what you want.

After a few weeks of repeating the program outlined here have passed, you should be more clear about what you want, which allows you to be more certain of what you want to record with your voice. You should now record a "wake up call" with six hours intervals, using the same sound of a normal call, and every time it rings in public, simply pretend you are picking a call from someone, go to an isolated place, and listen to your own voice recording. Your recording should contain whatever you wish to manifest by ending the following phrases:

- I think if I am not wealthy is because...
- I think being wealthier is better because...
- I think wealth can bring me suffering if...
- I think wealth can bring me happiness if...
- I think wealth can bring me love if...
- I think wealth can make me lonely if...
- I want a future with abundance next to a spouse who....
- I want a future with abundance and friends who....
- I want a future with abundance working on...
- I want to buy a house that has...

- I want to buy a car that...

- I want to travel to...

Step 8: Singing Mantras for Abundance

The purpose of this exercise consists in strengthening your self-confidence every day with the use of mantras. All you need to do is choose an element to focus on, either your hands or a buddhist bracelet, to count how many times you repeat each mantra.

You should pick one of the following mantras to repeat one hundred times a day:

- I love money and money loves me.

- God wants me wealthy and keeps sending me more money.

- God is always sending me good ideas to increase my profit.

- It is very easy to make money and I am getting wealthier.

- It is easy to become a millionaire.

- I am grateful for the twenty-thousand dollars I receive every month.

- I am grateful for the seventy-thousand dollars I receive every month.

- I am thankful for the perfect relationships I have today, for they reinforce my ability to become wealthy.

- I am thankful that I can earn enough money to travel to any country I want.

- I am thankful that I earn enough money to take the people I love to enjoy vacations.

- I feel joyful for having a happy life with many people who respect me and love to see me growing more abundant.

- I am grateful for the many rich friends that always teach me more about money.

- My work helps thousands of people who want to give me money for helping them.

- People see value in my work and always want to give me money.

- I receive millions of dollars every month because I help others.

- I receive thousands of dollars every month and unexpectedly.

- My business brings over five hundred thousand dollars to my life every year.

- Everything I do is a success.

- Everything I do brings more money to my life.

- My decisions bring me closer to wealth.

Step 9: Eliminating Negative Beliefs

At this point, you should already feel at a very positive state of mind in what regards attracting money. Nonetheless, I want to offer you another exercise, this time to eliminate any negative beliefs you may still have.

Part one:

- Think about the first time you felt that you would't be rich.

- Identify how old you were and what was occurring.

- Describe what you were seeing, touching, hearing, smelling or tasting.

- Who passed that energy and belief of scarcity to you?

- What is the emotion attached to it? Describe your feelings!

- Identity in which part of your body this energy feels stronger.

- Now pick a number from one to ten that describes the intensity of the emotion.

- Focus on that part of your body while praying to God for Divine healing.

- Repeat "heal me!", while imagining a white light cleaning that area of your body.

- Now pick a number from one to ten to evaluate if the feeling is gone.

- If the feeling of scarcity is gone, you will only keep a memory of it. Otherwise, repeat the exercise again, this time, by trying to find an earlier memory related to scarcity.

Part two:

Repeat the exercise mentioned above, for the following topics:

- In which moment in life you felt that you couldn't earn more?
- In which moment in life you felt that you shouldn't earn more?
- In which moment in life you felt that you were afraid to earn more?

Part three:

Answer the following questions based on your experience with the previous steps:

- What will it take for you to feel supported in obtaining more wealth?
- What will it take for you to attract more wealth?
- What will it take for you to get more wealth?

Part four:

Now test your results with the following exercise, and if the negative outcome is superior in value to the positive outcome, please repeat the whole system outlined in this book until you get a balance of 10 to your confidence and zero to your negative emotions.

Let's begin with the negative outcome:

- On a scale from 1 to 10, how high is the negative feeling about being wealthy?
- On a scale from 1 to 10, how high is the negative feeling about attracting money?

Now for the positive outcome:

- On a scale from 1 to 10, how high is your belief in your capacity to be wealthy?

- On a scale from 1 to 10, how high is your belief in your future as a millionaire?

Part five:

- On a scale from 1 to 10, how easily can you imagine yourself wearing expensive clothes?

- On a scale from 1 to 10, how easily can you imagine yourself driving an expensive car?

- On a scale from 1 to 10, how easily can you imagine yourself living in an expensive house?

- On a scale from 1 to 10, how easily can you imagine yourself seeing ten million dollars in your bank account?

Step 10: Cleaning Your Sexual Energy

One of the things that has always intrigued me is why so many business owners, millionaires and billionaires I met, use the word "fuck" so much. And upon further research, I came to an interesting conclusion. First, when people are struggling with their finances, their sexual desire decreases, and when they feel prosperous, their sexual desire increases. But why? The answer seems to be in the fact that, both money and sex, are forms of exchanging energy between human beings. It is then no coincidence that rich business owners claim to have a higher sex drive, and even women who are in management positions tend to want to cheat more often in their relationships. Furthermore, it is estimated that 53% of the wealthy men and 73% of the wealthy women have had extramarital affairs.

There are several other studies on this topic that are worth taking into consideration, although I will mention only two for the purpose of explaining this chapter.

First, and foremost, we have a study made on 30 thousand North Americans, with data collected over four decades, about the relationship between sex, happiness and money, led by Amy Muise — a social psychologist at the University of Toronto-Mississauga in Canada — published in the journal of *Social Psychological and Personality Science*. Interestingly, this study shows that there is a stronger correlation between sex and happiness than between sex and money, which may lead us to assume that the relation between sex and money is actually correlated to happiness, and can't exist without it. But this result is further complemented with another, this time obtained in Germany.

In a study conducted on "The Effect of Sexual Activity on Wages" it was found that people who have sex more than four times a week receive a 3.2 percent higher paycheck than those who have sex only once a week. The author, Nick Drydakis says that, "The outcome suggest that there is a positive relation between sexual activity and wages."

These studies add an important element that correlates with others, as "The theory concludes that people need to love and be loved (sexually and non-sexually) by others. In the absence of these elements, many people become susceptible to loneliness, social anxiety, and depression, which affect their working life."

In other words, sex affects our happiness which then reflects in our financial situation. And it was taking this data into consideration that the following list of question was created in order to erase your mental blocks related to sex.

Please recall a time when...

- Somebody richer than you wanted sex with you.
- Someone was happy to have sex with you.
- You were rejected because you wanted too much sex.
- You rejected someone because you couldn't be sexually pleased.
- You rejected an attractive person.
- You found you were adequate as a sexual partner.
- You found you could satisfy someone sexually.
- You were admired by your sexual qualities.
- You attracted beautiful partners for sex.
- You kept someone addicted to having sex with you.
- You were too sexual for someone.
- You were able to get away from someone who invalidated you sexually.
- You found you could get better sexual partners.

- You surprised yourself with your own endurance in attracting a partner.

- You discovered you did understand how to attract someone.

- You foresaw how sex should be acquired and arranged your life accordingly.

- You imagined yourself having sex with beautiful partners and worked towards making it happen.

- You did a masterpiece with yourself and became more attractive.

- You saw beautiful partners appearing in your life as you had imagined them.

- Your vision was complemented with more potential partners than you expected.

- You drew a plan to attract more sex into your life and followed it.

- You noticed somebody attracting a partner in the same way you do.

- You found somebody copying a mannerism you use to attract others.

- You adopted a mannerism from an attractive person.

- You made faces like an attractive person at yourself in the mirror.

- You decided to act completely different from an unattractive person.

- You decided to act in a similar way to an attractive person.

- You were classified as attractive by someone you weren't attracted to.

- You were classified as attractive by someone you were attracted to.

- Someone invited you for sex and you accepted.

- Someone invited you for sex and you rejected.

- You invited someone for sex and your invitation was accepted.

Step 11: Increasing Your Wealth by Using Karma

Once you start seeing money coming to your life, you need to understand that it's just a form of energy being materialized, and you need to keep this energy flowing by allowing it to flow.

In ancient times, because water was seen as valuable, money and water were both elements seen as interrelated. That's why so many palaces have both fountains and phallic symbols on display, in many cases phallic symbols represented in fountains or in the middle of artificial lakes. Water and money were both perceived as energies that needed to flow and be redirected in certain ways, in order to be obtained and appreciated in abundance.

Based on this principle, this exercise proposes you the same type of work.

First Step - Appreciation:

Once you notice that you are attracting more money than usual, enjoy it, by offering yourself a gift, such as a nice dinner, or short vacations. Treat yourself with a pleasant weekend where you can enjoy the benefits of your work. You should do this, at least, every two or three months. A weekend, relaxing by yourself or with your family in a new place, should be enough to make you feel prosperous and grateful for your accomplishments.

Second Step — Gratitude:

In this case, the source of your fortune is me, the author, even though I am merely manifesting the desires of the Creator, also known as God or Cosmic Consciousness. In order to be appreciative of the knowledge received, you basically need to give back the same gratitude in a material form. Although a simple "thank you" or a positive book review seems like a lot to ask for most people these days, which actually surprises me, for it shows how ungrateful they are when removed from their misery, such two examples are the minimum one should apply when being rescued from ignorance and guided towards more abundance.

A better form of gratitude, however, is demonstrated when you promote the survival of the one who shared his wisdom with you. And the only way to do this is through financial compensation, i.e., donations, further purchases of products created by the same person, or marketing promotions that increase the sales of this book.

In other words, once you realize that this book is making you much wealthier than you were, you can either donate ten percent of your new income to the author, promote this book to your friends and recommend them to buy it, or simply buy the entire collection authored by the same person. The more you help the author, the more he can continue helping the world, and in return, the more you open the gates of abundance for money to flow towards you by the same karmic law.

Step Three — Generosity:

The final stage is the world itself. The more money you make, using the method outlined here, the more you should contribute to the wellbeing of those who need help. In this case, I recommend contributing to different charities, orphanages, and also the animal protection institutions.

I don't recommend contributing to religious institutions and other intermediaries, because in most of these cases, you don't really know how the money is being invested.

I also don't recommend contributing to associations related to animal protection until you can be sure that they are investing your money wisely, because I have realized from personal experience that the large majority are a scam. I still remember how one day I rescued a dying seagull in the south of Portugal and contacted more than twenty different institutions related to animal protection, and they all ignored me through different types of replies that basically denied themselves any responsibility over the obvious. It was then, by talking about this issue with the local authorities, that I came to the conclusion that the associations for animal protection in Portugal are all a money laundry scam.

Surely, you should help children and unprotected animals the most, but in this vicious world, most of the money invested in donations doesn't end in the hands (or paws) of those who need it the most, and you're not helping yourself in any way, if failing to make sure that your money is properly invested.

If you can't be sure of how your money is helping someone, invest it yourself, as I often do, by buying toys for children and directly offer them yourself in a hospital or an institution that allows you to give such toys by hand.

A buddhist friend of mine used to do a very nice gesture to increase her positive karma. She would buy turtles and fishes, and other animals from local stores, and then set them free in their natural environment. Although you are keeping those business alive by paying for the animals, you are also using your money to rescue them, and that always increases your own flow of wealth, as if with each amount of money used to rescue animals, you increased the amount of money coming towards you. And she was indeed very well financially and always attracting jobs with very high salaries.

Step 12: Attracting More Wealth with Love

When you share love with the world, this love always comes back to you. Money is simply a means you use to experience such love in many more ways. Once you realize that using money to make others happier, or that buying the freedom of animals can increase your sense of self-worth, and how you feel about yourself, you will naturally want to make more. And that's how you become a better person while increasing your wealth at the same time.

As you can see, the belief that having money makes someone evil is a misinterpretation from religion and society in general. What makes one evil is the act of loving money, instead of what money can do for us and the world as a collective.

If you can understand how money can make you a better person, then, the richer you are, the more abundance you will be attracting, as you naturally see the positive outcome of having more.

That is the law of God and the Universe — abundance attracts abundance; and that abundance comes in the form of love and compassion, from which money is merely the material form we have to show it and apply it.

A person without money cannot do much for others. It is only the one who has more that can give more, and make a difference in this world.

This said, it is my personal desire that you use this book wisely and share your abundance with the rest of the world in a positive way.

About the Publisher

This book was published by the 22 Lions Bookstore.
For more books like this visit www.22Lions.com.
Join us on social media at:
Fb.com/22Lions;
Twitter.com/22lionsbookshop;
Instagram.com/22lionsbookshop;
Pinterest.com/22LionsBookshop.

www.ingramcontent.com/pod-product-compliance
Lightning Source LLC
Chambersburg PA
CBHW050438010526
44118CB00013B/1581